Tales from the Maryland Terrapins

Dave Ungrady

Sports Publishing L.L.C.
www.SportsPublishingLLC.com

Director of production: Susan M. Moyer
Project manager: Greg Hickman
Developmental editor: Gabe Rosen
Copy editors: Cynthia L. McNew and Holly Birch
Dust jacket design: Kerri Baker

ISBN: 1-58261-688-4

Printed in the United States.

SPORTS PUBLISHING L.L.C.
www.SportsPublishingLLC.com

To my wonderful wife Sharon,
whose support made the writing of this book possible.

Acknowledgments

Most of the inspiration for my writing this book comes from the athletes, coaches and friends whom I met and who have influenced, for good or bad, the way I have lived most of my life.

Thanks to Jim Dietsch, my soccer coach at Maryland, who let me be a part of a great team despite a season-long injury; the ever-amiable and entertaining Frank Costello, the head track coach; Stan Pitts, my running coach, whose trademark "Sooooeeey" call from across the track to provide motivation during workouts still echoes in my ear today; assistant track coach and later athletic director Dick Dull, for his kind heart; my first roommate Joe Bonelli, the Italian Stallion, who made college life entertaining; my second roommate Todd Hixson, whom I consider my fourth brother and the truest friend I have today; sprinter Manny Rosenberg, who taught me a sense of adventure that I will never forget; soccer teammate Dave Dorozinsky, a lifelong friend; and to all my track and soccer teammates, who helped provide memories worthy of two lifetimes. To Dave Fields, a great friend and avid Maryland fan who helped with the book, and to all the others who touched my life at Maryland to varying levels of significance—thanks for the good times and the bad. It was the best way to learn about life.

Contents

Foreword

by
Boomer Esiason

In January 1979, my not-so-spectacular high school football career at East Islip High School in Long Island was over and I had not received one scholarship offer to play college football. So I immersed myself in the high school basketball season.

In a game against our heated rival, West Islip, I managed to have one of my best and most satisfying games as a basketball player. We weren't the greatest team, and West Islip was one of the best in the state of New York that year. One of the best players for West Islip was Bill McFadden. He was also one of the most highly recruited football players at the time from Long Island. He could have picked Penn State, Syracuse or Virginia, but chose to attend Maryland.

We somehow won that game against West Islip that night in their gym, and my performance came at the right moment. Why? After the game my basketball coach told me that the University of Maryland coaches wanted to see me. My initial thought was, "What in the world is Lefty Driesell doing at my basketball game in West Islip?"

As I walked out of the locker room, I was shocked to see Tom Groom, a University of Maryland assistant football coach, who, from what I remember, was at the game to watch McFadden play. He said, "I had no idea you could run and are as athletic as you are." I told him that my high school football coach wouldn't let me run with the football because he thought I would get hurt.

Coach Groom then invited me to visit the Maryland campus. During my weekend visit, I developed food poisoning and saw little of the campus, other than the Adult Education Hotel & Conference Center, where I was staying. Still, that Sunday, to my complete surprise, head coach Jerry Claiborne offered me a scholarship.

Who could have known at that time what was about to happen during my four and a half years at Maryland?

My freshman year, I was a roommate with that kid from West Islip, Bill McFadden. I played junior varsity football that year, but I got a chance to suit up for a varsity game. During home games, Coach Claiborne picked one "zingo," an underclassman who normally would not dress for a varsity game, to do so. He picked me for the first game of the season, against Villanova at Byrd Stadium. I fully expected to play that game and was disappointed when I did not. That shows you how full of myself I was then.

I thought I was ready to play varsity my sophomore season. But I had read in the *Washington Post* that when summer practice started that year I was slated to be redshirted for the upcoming season. The coaches never told me ahead of time.

I was mad at the coaches, as well as disappointed and disillusioned. For the second consecutive season I found myself sitting in the students' section on game days, sometimes drinking Jack Daniel's and beers, instead of on the sidelines in my uniform, ready for action. I bitched, complained, felt sorry for myself, and practically flunked out of school.

After a tough summer session in 1981, I fought my way back academically and was positioned as the third-string quarterback heading into my second year of eligibility. Both Bob Milkovich and Brent Dewitz got injured in our opening game at Vanderbilt. Claiborne had no choice but to send in the maniac kid from Long Island the next week against West Virginia. I seized the opportunity and never looked back.

I owe a debt of gratitude to Claiborne and his coaching staff for sticking with me through the tough times. But it was athletic director Dick Dull's decision to hire Bobby Ross as our new head coach to replace Claiborne that more significantly affected my career. Dull's stroke of genius enabled Maryland's football program to become known as Quarterback U. in the 1980s.

Under the guidance of Ross, and his offensive coaching staff that included quarterback guru Joe Krivak and offensive line coach

Ralph Friedgen, young quarterbacks were given a system that utilized their strengths as prototypical pocket passers. Frank Reich, Stan Gelbaugh and I all went on to have successful collegiate and professional careers because of Ross. In the early to mid-1980s, a spotlight was shining on a new national football power: the University of Maryland.

My greatest memory while at Maryland came in a two-point victory over No. 3-ranked North Carolina in our final home game my senior year. In a nationally televised, hotly contested game, we won in the final minute. Thousands of fans stormed the field and carried us off in triumph. I definitely shed a tear that day. It was a resounding personal victory due to the long and bumpy road I had traveled. What made it special was the feeling of accomplishment that we, as a team, had finally brought Maryland football back to where it once had been—a national power.

Most importantly, I was fortunate to go to a school such as Maryland that provided a great learning environment for academics and life in general. It was big and competitive and had everything I needed to help me grow.

The people you meet in college are a big part of your life. There were so many people who were good to me and made me the player and person that I became. I often feel extremely fortunate that I had the chance to attend Maryland. With a little luck, I was able to fight through some difficult times. Still, when I think of those days, as tough as they were at times, they don't compare with the hardships endured by someone like my son Gunner, who battles with cystic fibrosis.

Maryland helped me grow up and mature. From that first game when I dressed as a zingo to the last game when I was carried off the field as a hero, those days at Maryland played a big part in making me who I am today.

Love and Maryland Athletics

Colonel Tom Fields sat across the restaurant table from his youngest son, Dave, and me, reminiscing about his magnificent Maryland career during the chatty lunch session. We were all runners at one time for the University of Maryland. The colonel was one of Maryland's first national-caliber runners, in the late 1930s and early 1940s, and later was a Marine Corps commander.

Dave and I were teammates in the late 1970s. He was a steady contributor to the cross-country program; I was an All-Conference middle distance runner and a captain of the track team in 1980.

During that late winter day in 2003, the 84-year-old colonel wore a black windbreaker emblazoned with "University of Maryland Athletics" in gold on the left chest. He also wore a ring given to him and former teammate Jim Kehoe as top Maryland athletes one year. The ring had lost some of its clarity and luster. The lettering had softened, and it was difficult to comprehend the reason for the dull-sculpted image of a woman standing alone. What was she holding in her hand?

Those minor cosmetic flaws didn't matter. The ring still radiated surreal symbolism when you thought of what it meant to the colonel and its place in the history of University of Maryland athletics. Pride poured out of its pores, more so when the always engaging elder Fields told the story about the ring and his marriage.

The ring was the only one on any of the colonel's fingers, prompting his son to ask him for the first time, "Dad, where's your wedding ring?"

"Ahhhhhh," the colonel growled, a sign he was about to shift into recollection mode.

He had been dating Patricia, his future wife, for one year. In 1952, at the age of 34, it was time for the suave socialite to trade in his lady-chasing shoes. A second running career was about to end. He and his wife-to-be talked about wedding rings. She asked him if he wanted one.

"No," he told her. "I've got a ring."

The colonel's new love, one that would yield four children and a golden wedding anniversary, was not his first love. The colonel's first love, his lifelong mistress—the University of Maryland—radiated red and white and glowed black and gold. It gave him a lifetime of tremendous memories as an elite athlete. It provided the backdrop for his legacy as the first athletic fundraiser of impact at the school, the commander of the school's fundraising group that financially helps drive athletics at the school today. It is a love that is still strong and one that has comfortably complemented the love for his wife.

The colonel has been married 51 years. He's been in love with the University of Maryland for more than 60 years. Can a man be more blessed than to have two such strong and lingering loves in his life?

2

The Early Years:
War Influence Fades, Athletics Begin

The dawn of athletics at the University of Maryland dates back to around the time of the Civil War, when informal baseball and football games were played at Maryland Agricultural College, which opened in 1856.

Interest in athletics between schools grew slowly, in part because the U.S. War Department opposed intercollegiate athletics. The department felt physical education at the schools rivaled military training. But military influence eventually waned.

Baseball and Buck

The first recorded intercollegiate game in the history of the school was in 1888, when Maryland's baseball team faced a team of students from St. John's College and the Naval Academy in Annapolis, Maryland. Some records say M.A.C. played St. John's in the morning and the Naval Academy in the afternoon and that M.A.C. won at least one of the games. The baseball team's first official year was 1893, when it finished the season with a 1-5 record.

Like other athletic teams at Maryland during the late 19th and early 20th century, the baseball team was a varsity club that played mostly local colleges, high schools and amateur teams. Coaches and managers were students and played on the teams.

One player stood out during that period. Infielder Charles "Buck" Herzog was also the team manager before he left M.A.C. in 1905. The Baltimore native played in the majors for six teams from 1908 to 1920. He won at least three pennants with the New York Giants and also managed that team.

Football's Early Follies

In 1890, a football team composed mostly of M.A.C. students lost to two local high schools in Maryland, Sandy Spring and Laurel. The college did not officially recognize the team, but they did not forbid the team from using the school's name. The players provided their own uniforms.

The team of 1890 featured 11 men playing 60-minute games. With the same number of players and two new additions to the roster, M.A.C. played three games in 1891. It is unclear who won the first two games against Hyattsville and Gallaudet. But there's no question who won the third game. M.A.C. beat Sandy Spring on Thanksgiving Day, prompting the school to formally organize an athletic association the following year.

Wrong Way Shorty

Pearse "Shorty" Prough, the fleet Aggies halfback, performed a dubious feat in the Episcopal game that first season. After recovering an Episcopal fumble, he ran the wrong way for 30 yards, then reversed his field and ended up with a 35-yard net gain. Apparently it was the team's only positive yardage of the game.

When contacted later to reflect on the play, Prough said one more block from a teammate on his run would have resulted in an M.A.C. touchdown. Episcopal High's *Monthly Chronicle* wrote that Maryland's play "showed an unaccreditable ignorance of football."

Champions or Cheaters

In 1893, the Aggie football team turned things around, winning its first championship and finishing the year 6-0. The Aggies beat two high schools, a club team and three colleges. M.A.C. shut out its first four opponents. The Aggies were District of Columbia champions and won the collegiate championship of Maryland with wins over Johns Hopkins, St. John's and Western Maryland, but not without a little controversy.

The win over St. John's was perhaps the most dramatic of the season. With the Aggies ahead 6-0 and possessing the ball on St. John's 25-yard line, St. John's walked off the field 20 minutes into the second half, claiming a referee had made a bad decision. Here's how St. John's described the incident in a response they wrote in the *Baltimore American* newspaper three days after the game:

"At an early period of the game, when the St. John's team was within 15 yards of their adversary's goal, a decision by which the M.A.C. were allowed to score the only touchdown made by the quarterback after a run of 90 yards, with no one in pursuit, appeared a very doubtful one. After this the wranglings and objections were the principal factors introduced in the game, obviously to cause delay and waste time…"

Another account written in a Maryland publication 21 years later offered a different scenario that led to the touchdown. "…when M.A.C., aided by half the student body, shoved the ball over the goal line, St. John's left the field, and not without cause, as the finish of the game was, to say the least, unseemly."

The writer of that story also said the star of St. John's was a professional wrestler. St. John's later claimed they won the championship of Maryland after they beat Warren Athletic Club of Wilmington, Del.

The Dawn of the M.I.F.A., Hired Players, and Homered by Georgetown

In 1894, Skinner, the team quarterback in 1892, spearheaded the formation of the Maryland Intercollegiate Football Association to avoid future confusion about who was the state champion. In addition to M.A.C., the association included Western Maryland, Johns Hopkins, Washington College and Baltimore City College.

With the Aggies returning 11 starters from their championship team, hopes were high that year to successfully defend the title. They shut out their first two opponents, scoring 52 points in their first game against Western Maryland.

M.A.C. next faced St. John's. No ill will erupted on the field in St. John's 22-6 victory. According to this portion of a report in the *Baltimore American*: "The game was…marked by gentlemanly good feeling…There was no wrangling amongst the players, nor with the umpires, and no slugging."

But this was, after all, M.A.C. vs. St. John's, a rivalry that was beginning to breed consistent controversy. The *Mountain Echo*, the student publication of Mt. St. Mary's College, claimed St. John's hired "two or three" players from Lehigh University to play against the Aggies. The report said M.A.C. protested the game.

The season's in-game drama would not end there. After the St. John's game, M.A.C. was scheduled to play Johns Hopkins at National Park in Washington, D.C., site of the old Griffith Stadium. A large crowd showed up to watch the Aggies, but John Hopkins did not make it to the game. A phone call confirmed that the Baltimore school had canceled the game, prompting another call from Maryland asking Georgetown's junior varsity team to show up on short notice. They did, with seven varsity players.

With a 6-4 lead, the Aggies refused to continue play when they felt it became too dark. The referee then ruled Georgetown the winner by forfeit. The referee was none other than Big Mike Mahoney, Georgetown's varsity halfback.

Elder Statesmen

Many of the players on M.A.C.'s early football teams were older than the other students, and it was difficult for the team to find opponents at first. The schedule during its first quarter-century of play included mostly local colleges, including Georgetown, Navy and Western Maryland College, as well as several local high schools. Its strongest rivalry was against Johns Hopkins.

Some coaches played on the team, and they occasionally recruited neighborhood thugs to play on the team.

School support for football thrived during those early days. Students, faculty and alumni began to flock to games. Students and faculty formed an athletic association, and professors helped pay for real uniforms. A $5,000 personal note from a member of the school's board of trustees helped build a new gymnasium in 1893. At about that time, stories about college sports started appearing in the sports pages of newspapers.

Adoption of the school's colors happened at around this time. When a dental department professor won a prize at a state exhibition for showing a set of plates made of maroon and black rubber, University teams adopted those colors.

Incoming freshmen received a pamphlet of University cheers to memorize, including this one:

Rif! Raf! Ruf!
Rif! Raf! Ruf!
University of Maryland!
Is pretty hot stuff!

Football Put on Hold

In 1895, Maryland's new commandant of cadets stalled any momentum the football program had gained from the previous season. The commandant, Lieutenant Clough Overton, felt there was no place for football in the curriculum of a college. He cut off the funds for football equipment, and he sternly enforced his order that all students be bathed, shaved and in uniform by the start of the 6:00 p.m. supper formation.

That restriction shortened football practice to 45 minutes. The team captain then asked for a delayed supper formation for the team, a courtesy offered the players the previous four years. The lieutenant denied the request. The players felt they would be at a severe disadvantage against competitors and decided not to field a team that year.

Gridiron Squad Rebuilds

The Aggies, agitated and assertive, regrouped in 1896. Only two starters returned from the team of 1894. One of them, fullback Greenville Lewis, was elected captain and coach. From the outset, he took firm control as a strict disciplinarian of his forces.

Lewis did not allow any contact work the first month of practice. Instead, he put the players through calisthenics, running, dummy scrimmages and blackboard instruction. He gathered the team an hour before reveille each morning for a 10-mile run. When football drills began, the players faced a field made up mostly of gravel.

Lewis banned smoking, drinking and pie eating during the football season. He dismissed the fastest man on the team, halfback Charley Cabrera, for smoking.

Some players were unhappy with the move and tried to have Lewis removed by forming an athletic committee to run the team. But the coach convinced the school to keep him on board.

The school's students responded to Coach Lewis with enthusiasm. Some joined the football players for the early-morning 10-mile run. They bought him a pearl gray and maroon sweater before the first game against Eastern High. Still, Maryland lost the game, 6-0. But Maryland ended the season with six wins, two losses and two ties, although six of the games were played against high schools.

Darkness Falls

The Aggies faced the University of Maryland-Baltimore in Baltimore in the last game of the 1896 football season to determine the state championship. With minutes remaining and the game scoreless, Maryland had charged downfield to their opponent's two-yard line, but suddenly they found trouble advancing the ball.

The referee called the game because of darkness before the Aggies could score. Maryland players figured out why they had such a tough time crossing the goal line. Maryland-Baltimore had lined up 14 players against the Aggies. The extra three players had snuck on as darkness set in.

Lewis, the Aggies coach and captain, asked the referee to give M.A.C. the win, but the referee refused. However, Maryland-Baltimore's players voted two days later to concede the game and the state championship to the Aggies.

The Return of Hopkins Signals Bad Times

M.A.C.'s state championship in 1896 was, in a sense, incomplete. The Aggies did not play powerful rival Johns Hopkins, who did not field a team that year.

Hopkins did return in 1897 and beat M.A.C. 30-6 in the third game of the season. That began a string of four successive defeats for the Aggies, who had started the season with two wins over high school teams. They finished the year 2-4.

The Aggies failed to post a winning season during the next five campaigns. It was so bad in 1899 that the team cancelled the season after winning just one of its first five games.

First Paid Coach Fills In on the Field

M.A.C. hired D. John Markey as its first football coach in 1902 for a fee of $300 for the season. His first team improved by two wins over the previous season. Markey brought a fitness program back to the team for the first time since Greenville ran his boot camp in 1896. After practice each player ran a mile, finishing with a 100-yard sprint. He is also credited with using a tackling dummy for the first time at the school.

Markey hadn't planned to play for Maryland during his first year as head coach. But fullback Ed Brown decided not to play in the season-opening loss against Georgetown after a Georgetown supporter threatened to kill him, and Markey filled in for the frightened fullback. Maryland adopted a "football policy" that allowed Markey to play in games outside of Maryland. Still, the Aggies lost 27-0.

Football's eligibility rules in the early 1900s were ambiguous at best. M.A.C. tried to do something about that and wrote a philosophy on football. The school said it would clean up athletics and would offer "no inducements to any athlete."

A Loose Hold on Track

The school's yearbook, *Reveille,* reported that up until about 1902, the track men did not take their activity seriously. "They had conceived the idea that training for the track team consisted of substituting the pipe for the cigarette and of eating no more than three square meals a day. Their ambition seemed to be satisfied by running around the track a few times on each annual field day and it apparently had never occurred to them to attend any general meets outside of the College."

To inspire more dedication in the track athlete, the school's athletic committee arranged a series of records that had to be surpassed before a medal would be given in field day competitions.

That year, the yearbook reported that a "Captain Turner" broke the college record in the 220-yard dash and the quarter-mile. *The Reveille* said a "great deal of interest" was taken in the track team of 1902 and that the team "made a name for itself" at the Georgetown meet in which Captain Turner broke the two records.

Water Training

Running track at M.A.C. in the early 1900s was quite an adventure. *Reveille* reported that "the only available running course was a cinder path that led from the college to the Experiment Station ... and this path contains cinders of all sizes from molecules to masses. It is especially adapted to spraining ankles and skinning knees."

There was a quarter-mile track, but it was for the most part inaccessible. *The Reveille* writes, "The greater part of the year this is under water, presenting a magnificent circular canal. All this adds to the scenic effect of the landscape, but has no particular advantage as a running track. It is ready for us about the first of June, affording opportunity for two weeks of practice during the nine months of the college term."

Traveling Woes

A football game against Washington College in 1902 typified the traveling woes of the time. The team left College Park at 6:30 a.m. en route to Chestertown, Maryland. They boarded a train to Washington, another train to Baltimore, and still another to Havre de Grace. Then the Aggies rode a slow ferry to the Eastern Shore and a horse-drawn vehicle to Chestertown, 18 miles away. Maryland missed lunch and had just enough time to dress for the game. They returned to College Park at 9:00 p.m., ending a journey that included a 0-0 tie.

Markey's best season during his three years as M.A.C.'s head coach came in 1903. He guided the Aggies to a 7-4 record, with wins over Western Maryland and the University of Maryland in Baltimore. But they suffered shutout losses to area rivals Georgetown and St. John's.

In the last game of the season against Columbian University, each team featured pro players—fullback Granville Church for Columbian and Markey for Maryland. Columbian complained first about Markey, but they backed down after Maryland mentioned Church's status. Both teams agreed to let their stars play. Markey scored the winning touchdown in the 6-0 game.

Markey's momentum did not last long. Upset over no increase in what he considered a meager salary, he coached the Aggies part-time in 1904, and Maryland struggled to a 2-4-2 record.

Students Want Athletic Options

Markey's struggles on the football field in part led to the beginning of basketball at M.A.C. Students wanted more athletic competitions after the football season. In 1905, 14 years after Dr. James Naismith invented the game in Massachusetts, each company at the school practiced for two weeks to prepare for three games against other school companies, for a total of six games. Company "C" came out on top and won a silk banner that symbolized winning the championship.

The tournament created enough excitement to form an All-College team, which lost games to the Washington YMCA and Carroll Institute. The basketball season ended abruptly when the basketball players started their track and baseball seasons in the spring.

Basketball continued primarily as an intra-campus activity for nearly the next two decades. The team played games against other colleges three more seasons through 1922, winning four out of 30 games. It was not officially recognized as an intercollegiate sport at the school until 1923.

The Perseverance of Curley Byrd

M.A.C. managed winning records in football during its next two seasons. More important, 1905 marked the emergence of Harry "Curly" Byrd, whom many consider the father of Maryland athletics.

Curley Byrd

First-year coach Fred K. Nielsen, a former halfback from the University of Nebraska, tolerated the $300-a-year salary because he worked with the State Department. Nielsen took up to two hours of annual leave per day during the season to coach the team.

Nielsen's two-year tenure was considered a success—he had a combined record of 11-7-0—but he started his career with a near blunder. When the 16-year-old Harry "Curley" Byrd showed up to claim equipment, Nielsen told him to go play with the kids, that football is a man's game.

Byrd's father wanted his curly-haired son to study law at Dickinson College. But Harry wanted to be an engineer and opted for M.A.C. And he wanted to play football, despite his father's warning not to do so.

Despite the initial rejection, Byrd persisted. He purchased a pair of women's stockings, bought his own football shirt and pants, and made his own cleats. (One version of the story says he nailed pieces of leather to his oldest shoes to make cleats; another says he had a shoemaker nail some cleats to an old pair of brogans, a sturdy ankle-high work shoe.) One historical account said Byrd wore those same pants throughout his five-year career at Maryland.

Byrd made his debut toward the end of the third game of the season against heavily favored Navy. The Aggies lost 17-0, but Byrd was so impressive that he kept his starting position the rest of the season. And he won the ultimate praise of his father. "Since you're going to play football, I'm glad you're doing it well," he wrote to his son.

Papa Terp

Football captured the most attention of all Maryland teams through the early 1900s. And Byrd, more than anyone else, most influenced the development of the program in the first half of the 21st century.

He is arguably the most influential figure in the school's history. Byrd helped shape the school's athletic policy as football head coach for 23 years and athletic director from 1914 to 1936. He formed the foundation for the school's growth, serving as president for 18 years after having been an assistant to the president and vice president.

Millard Tydings, a U.S. Senator from Maryland and a 1910 Maryland graduate, called Byrd the father of the University of Maryland in a newspaper story about Byrd.

Byrd was considered the top athlete during his time as a student at M.A.C. He competed in football, baseball and track and field. Byrd was called a "brainy" athlete, and his build was described as "compact." He was a leading pitcher on the baseball team and the top sprinter on the track team. At times Byrd was the leadoff and anchorman of the relay team, and he departed M.A.C. as the school record holder in the 50, 100 and 220-yard dashes. He ran the 100 yards in 10 seconds, the 50 yards in 5.2 seconds, the 440 in 52 seconds and the 220 in 22.3 seconds.

Byrd used his swiftness to dominate play on the football field, where he earned most of his athletic notoriety. During his second season on the football team in 1906, Byrd also played quarterback, and he scored twice in the last game of the season to lead Maryland to its biggest win that year, 35-0 over Washington College. Maryland finished the season 5-3.

Charles Melick, who worked in the school's agricultural experiment station, took over as head coach in 1907. Melick hired kicking specialist and Washington attorney Durant Church as an assistant coach. Church was credited with teaching Byrd the proficiencies of kicking, adding another role to the end/quarterback.

Byrd also helped with coaching that year because Melick and Church were too busy with work to dedicate full-time hours to coaching M.A.C. The Aggies struggled that year, finishing 3-6, including a 5-0 loss to Gallaudet in the last game of the season. On the last play of his Maryland career in that game, Byrd ran 90 yards for a touchdown, but the play was nullified due to a penalty.

A Busy Byrd

Byrd returned to Maryland in 1911 to coach the football team and teach English and history. He became basketball and baseball coach in 1913, roles he served until 1923. He was named assistant to the school's president in 1918 while he was also serving as athletic director.

In that role, Byrd helped unify the Maryland Agricultural College with the Baltimore School to form the University of Maryland. In 1921, Byrd named the student newspaper *The Diamondback* after the breed of turtle that was indigenous to the wetlands of the state of Maryland.

Byrd was one of the founding fathers of the M-Club in 1923 and was the club's first president. Meanwhile, in 1933 he helped adopt the Diamondback Terrapin as the school's mascot. Clearly, no one has done as much as Curley Byrd to help develop athletics at Maryland.

Shipley "Does Somethin'"

It was another new coach and another struggling season for the Aggies' football team in 1908. They finished the season 3-8 and were shut out in seven games under coach Bill Lang. With the same coach in 1909, the Aggies finished 2-5. But there was one bright spot to that season. Burton Shipley debuted as quarterback during the third game of the season and threw the pass for the game-winning touchdown.

A resident of College Park since the age of four, Shipley first experienced M.A.C. athletics as a water boy for the 1896 football team. He later was captain of the football, basketball and baseball teams at M.A.C. and earned 16 letters in those sports during six years at the school. Rather than go to high school, Shipley completed a year at the M.A.C. prep school and another in the sub-freshman course. He was an All-State quarterback in 1911 and is considered the best third baseman to play for Maryland.

After serving in World War I, Shipley became the athletic director and coach at the University of Delaware. He returned to Maryland in 1923 to coach Maryland's basketball and baseball teams.

Shipley resigned as basketball coach in 1947 with a 243-199 record in 24 seasons. In 37 years of coaching Maryland baseball, Shipley produced four major league players: Louis "Bosey" Berger (Cleveland Indians), Charles Keller (Yankees, Tigers), Harold Keller (Senators) and Sherry Robertson (Senators).

The "Ship" was known for a colorful personality, but he became flustered whenever anyone created a fuss over him. He often was heard uttering the phrase, "I say, I say."

"His sense of humor stimulates all those with whom he associates on campus," wrote *The Baltimore Sun* in 1951.

A fan once hit him in the head with a water bag. "I remember a time they got rowdy during one game," said Shipley, in the book *Maryland Basketball: Red, White and Amen.* "Things weren't going so well. Somebody yelled through the quiet, 'Do somethin', Ship!'" Shipley's daughter later named a racehorse after the expression.

Late in his career as Maryland basketball coach, Shipley chased Tommy Mont into the locker room after the player made a mistake that cost the team a game. The players led him in to the shower and turned the water on the coach, saying, "You're all wet, Ship."

After Shipley was ejected from his final game as Maryland's baseball coach, he sat down on a chair outside the dugout and refused to leave the field. The umpire let him remain in the stadium that still bears his name.

In another game, Shipley called a timeout after a Maryland player dropped a fly ball that Shipley thought should have caught. He left the dugout with a fungo bat and, upon reaching the player, hit fly balls at him. The game resumed when Shipley returned to the dugout.

When Shipley coached his last team at Maryland in 1960, he left behind dozens of profound memories as one of the more prominent athletic figures in the university's history.

Tooth Collecting Can Cost a Team a Win

The second decade of the 1900s was one of the more successful in Maryland football history. New head coach Royal Alston, the captain and tackle of the 1909 George Washington team, led the Aggies to four wins and a tie in its first five games.

The Aggies were fortunate to tie Johns Hopkins in the third game of the season. Hopkins faced second down with two yards needed for a first down, on Maryland's eight-yard line with three minutes to play. When a Hopkins guard ran off the field to the bench, the referee penalized the team 10 yards. Apparently, the guard wanted to keep as a memento a tooth that had been knocked out on the previous play. Hopkins could not convert a first down, and Maryland blocked the ensuing field goal that would have won the game for Hopkins.

The victory helped the Aggies finish the season with a winning record, 4-3-1.

Byrd to the Rescue

In 1911, another new head coach, Charley Donnely, did not last the entire season. He gave up control of the team with a 2-4-1 record. At that point, injures had reduced the number of healthy players on the Aggies' roster. They did not have even enough to scrimmage the varsity eleven.

That grim scenario ultimately led to one of the more fortuitous moments in the school's football history. The Aggies invited local high school teams to serve as scrimmage opponents in practice.

One was Western High School in Georgetown, where Harry "Curly" Byrd was the football, track and baseball coach. It was an easy decision for Byrd; of course he would help the boys at his alma mater.

The technique of Byrd's boys was so impressive that the Aggies signed him to help prepare M.A.C. for its last two games of the season. Maryland narrowly beat Western Maryland (6-0) and Gallaudet (6-2).

writers that the combination between quarterback Gus Dorais and running back Knute Rockne at Notre Dame pioneered the forward pass.

The school hired Byrd as a part-time coach for football, baseball, and track for $400 a year. He also started writing sports for *The Washington Star* newspaper, a job he performed until 1932.

Maryland initially offered Byrd $300 to coach the football team. Byrd wanted $1200. Maryland agreed, requiring Byrd to work nine months of the year, coach football, baseball, basketball, track, and teach English and history.

A Man of Persuasion and Vision

Byrd did not smoke, curse, or drink alcohol, and he often studied the Bible. He was an idea man and a dreamer. Many of his visions extended beyond baseball.

In the book *The Terrapins*, Paul Attner wrote about a man who saw Byrd sitting on a hill on campus before he was the football coach. He asked Byrd was he was doing.

"I'm drawing a sketch of M.A.C. as it will be someday," said Byrd. The man, Dr. Levin Broughton, claims the campus resembles the images Byrd drew that day.

Byrd's style was to be more the encouraging teacher than critical coach. "He never yelled in practice or a at a game," said one of Byrd's players, Geary "Swede" Eppley, in the book *The Terrapins*. "He pointed out mistakes and explained what you did wrong. He took a calm approach. The strongest thing he'd say was 'for cripes sake.' Shipley, one of Byrd's first quarterbacks, remembered how Byrd would dress in the same room with the players even 20 years after he was coach.

Byrd practiced the following philosophy. "If you can't lead 'em, lick 'em. If you can't lick 'em, join 'em. And if you can't join 'em, seduce 'em." H.L. Mencken wrote the following about Byrd for *The Baltimore Sun* newspaper: "The thing to do with a man of such talents is not to cuss him for doing his job as well; it is far wiser, so long as hanging him is unlawful, to give him a bigger and better one."

Things Get Better with Byrd

Before 1912, when the school had 130 undergraduate students, prep school football teams constantly beat Maryland's school of "farmers," as they were called. Johns Hopkins considered Maryland only a practice game. The only athletic facility was a bare field at the foot of a hill, and there was no athletic dressing room. Athletes dressed in one of four buildings on campus and shared one shower.

Byrd's first year as head coach helped to ultimately change that environment. The Aggies finished the 1912 season with a 6-1-1 record, losing only to St. John's of Maryland.

Byrd had almost lost his quarterback, Shipley, before the season began. Shipley was frustrated with the military aspect of college life and had departed M.A.C. Over dinner, Byrd asked Shipley what he would do if Byrd would arrange for the quarterback to not have to take part in drill anymore. While contemplating the question, Shipley said Byrd had ordered him a plank steak, a piece of meat he had never eaten before. The move helped persuade Shipley to stay for two more years.

Helping with Hoops

Shipley also helped Byrd develop basketball at M.A.C. As a guard on the team during Byrd's first year as head coach in 1913, he helped M.A.C. finish the season with a 6-5 record. The program was plagued with inadequate facilities and equipment, prompting Byrd to start a campaign for a new basketball arena.

Basketball at M.A.C. received a boost when it joined the District Intercollegiate League in 1917. But the Aggies had little success in games played at the Washington YMCA against Catholic, George Washington and Gallaudet. Students viewed basketball as a diversion between the fall and spring sports, which still reigned supreme at M.A.C., and a sense of apathy toward the sport prevailed for the next few years. After five consecutive losses in 1919, basketball became an insignificant part of campus life.

Give Me a Football Player or Give Me Death

Fortunately for Byrd, students strongly supported his football team even as he was trying to help build the basketball team.

Byrd did not believe in recruiting athletes, and he refused to help them as other schools did. He also scheduled games against far superior opponents. "We always used to schedule four or five schools every year we had no right beating," said Jack Faber, who played and coached under Byrd at M.A.C., in *The Terrapins: Maryland Football*. "He liked the challenge. We were usually outnumbered."

Few high schools in Maryland played football, and most of Byrd's athletes had no previous experience when they came to College Park. Byrd was fond of saying, "I'll make a football player out of him or I'll die trying."

With Byrd establishing stability at the head coach position, Maryland posted winning records through 1920. During that period, Maryland enjoyed four glorious wins over rival Johns Hopkins, including a 54-0 Thanksgiving Day romp in 1916. They also beat Hopkins 14-0 in 1919 in front of 15,000 fans, the largest crowd at a Maryland football game up to that point. They also lost big twice in 1917, 62-0 to Navy and 57-0 against Penn State. Wisely, Maryland did not play Penn State again until 1937.

Fleet Feet, Strong Foot

The 1916 season was noted for a world-class sprinter who developed into a great kicker and for Maryland playing a team beyond the Maryland and Virginia borders for the first time. Also that year, the school's name was changed to Maryland State College.

In the summer of 1915, 16-year-old Edward Brewer ran the 100-yard dash in 9.8 seconds, tying the world record. Nicknamed "Untz," Brewer joined Maryland the following year. He was noted as much for his punting and field goal kicking ability as for his fleetness of foot. In a game against V.M.I., Brewer kicked an 80-yard punt.

In its first game against an opponent outside of Maryland and Virginia, the Aggies beat New York University 10-7 on a winning field goal by Brewer. Brewer also returned the opening kickoff for a score in Maryland's next game, the rout of Johns Hopkins.

The First World War greatly affected the teams of 1917 and 1918. Walter "Big Boy" Posey would have played his sixth season for the Aggies if he had not been called in to defend his country. With fewer than the normal number of players, the Aggies reduced the 1918 season to six games. That year, Byrd added to his duties as head coach and athletic director, becoming an assistant to the president.

Brewer, a war veteran, was expected to return to Maryland for another season of greatness. But he opted instead to work that year in a U.S. government job. The highlight of Maryland's season of mediocrity—a 5-4 record—was its 14-0 away victory over Johns Hopkins in front of 15,000 fans.

One war veteran who did play for Maryland in 1919 was running back Leroy Mackert, whom Brewer persuaded to attend the school. A former tackle, the 6'2", 193-pound Mackert was some load. In his first game as in 1919, Mackert ran over four Catholic players, forcing all of them out of the game.

Mackert was 25 when he entered Maryland. He had played two years for Lebanon Valley College before the war. On Sundays, he played pro football, something the better players commonly did at that time. Francis Stan, a columnist for *The Washington Evening Star*, credited Mackert as being one of several people who helped develop pro football.

National Notice

Byrd helped Maryland's football team rise from local power to regional notoriety in the 1920s. Maryland managed two upset wins over Yale, one of the best teams in the country, and other wins over Princeton, Pennsylvania, Syracuse, Cornell and North Carolina.

With a stronger reputation on the football field, the Aggies stretched their competitive legs, playing more teams outside Maryland and Virginia. In the 1920 season, Maryland faced Syracuse and North Carolina for the first time and won both games.

Brewer and his reliable boot returned to Maryland that season. He kicked a 36-yard field goal to win games against national power Syracuse and averaged more than 60 yards on seven punts. It was considered Maryland's most significant victory to date. After the game, students built a bonfire in College Park that could be seen for miles. Some students even drove down to Washington, where they celebrated the victory in the streets.

Geary Eppley, an end, broke his nose in the Syracuse game. It "was splattered all over my face," he says in *The Terrapins: Maryland Football.* "Nobody, including us, expected us to win as we did." Losses to first-time opponents Princeton and Rutgers from New Jersey were the only defeats of the season for the Aggies.

Basketball Gets a Boost

While Maryland's football team was gaining regional attention, its basketball team was getting its second wind as interest in college basketball increased in parts of the U.S.

Maryland State joined the NCAA in 1919 and two years later became a charter member of the Southern Intercollegiate Conference, which became the Southern Conference in 1923. In 1920, the Atlanta Athletic Club staged its first basketball tournament, which is considered the forerunner of the current ACC basketball tournament.

With a booming economy following World War I, the demand for leisure activity grew. In June, 1922, Maryland announced it would build a gymnasium, complete with a balcony and skylight.

Byrd's Namesake Stadium

In 1923, concern was raised about the negative effects of athletics on academics. In April of that year, a meeting was called to discuss adhering to rules for academic standing established by the Southern Conference. A reference was made in *The Diamondback* to the "negligible" benefits of taking nine credit hours per semester. There were some concerns about the extensive travels of the football team.

Travel of alumni when they returned to campus to watch games was one reason Byrd in 1915 had asked the school for $12,000 to build a new stadium. He wanted a new field, a training area and a place to also house athletes. The stadium, named after the coach, was completed in 1923 at a cost of $60,000. It was built for 5,000 spectators, but could be expanded to accommodate 5,000 more. It also included the first real locker rooms in Maryland's history.

Maryland played its first game in new Byrd stadium that season in the home opener against Randolph Macon. In a symbolic tribute to their coach, the Aggies won handily, 53-0.

The stadium was officially dedicated to Byrd during the last home game of the season, a 40-6 triumph of Catholic. During a brief halftime ceremony, Byrd told the story of the captain of a ship, who, on being congratulated by the owner for bringing the vessel into port through a terrific storm, said "Oh, hell" and walked away. As *The Diamondback* said, "This was interpreted to mean that a fellow is expected to do his best and let it go at that."

Byrd Stadium looks different than it did in 1923. Upper decks on the far sideline were part of the changes made to the stadium in 1990.

The Debut of the M-Club

Intended or not, the beginning of the M-Club created a feeling of good will toward and among athletes at the school at a time when questions surfaced about the significance of athletics at the school.

One of the reasons eight former Maryland athletes founded the club was to promote courtesy and fair play by the athletes. The other reasons were to promote amateurism and spectator decorum and to host officials and guests.

The club organized the school's first homecoming, which included freshman and varsity football games, a noon luncheon, a pep rally, a march to the stadium, and an alumni dinner and dance. One hundred of a possible 250 letter winners attended the club's organizational meeting that day. Those who had earned a varsity letter could join the club for $1. Today, the M-Club's membership fee is $30 and boasts some 1200 members of a possible 4100 letter winners.

Nappy and Zeke Test the Elis

During the 1923 season, Byrd hired two former M.A.C. stars as his assistants, bruising defensive back Country Morris and six-year quarterback Burton Shipley. Surrounded by inspiration and familiarity, Byrd's squad ended the season 7-2-1.

The second game that season produced perhaps the most profound result. A fully healthy Aggies team traveled to Franklin Field to face two-time national champion Penn, one of the founding football schools. A field goal by Johnny "Boots" Groves in the final couple minutes of play was all Maryland needed to forge the upset in front of 40,000 fans.

Such games create legacies. Newspapers said quarterback Kirk Besley ran the team like Napoleon in moleskin. He was thus nicknamed Nappy. End Bill "Zeke" Supplee, whose soft basketball-playing hands made him a threat as a receiver, made the Associated Press All-American team for his play against Penn and later against Yale. He was the first Maryland player to receive the honor.

Against Yale that same year, Maryland scored on its first two possessions while holding the Elis to no first downs during the first quarter. Maryland led 14-12 at halftime, but lost the game 16-14. They felt they should have won the game. A referee ruled a 38-yard drop kick by Grove in the fourth period did not go through the uprights. Byrd said it was good by a "country mile." One player on the field, running back George Heine, said it flew inside the goal posts by eight feet.

Byrd claimed the loss to Yale in front of 20,000 spectators at the Yale Bowl provided his greatest thrill in sports. "I do not believe [two feats] ever have been matched against a high ranking eleven in the history of football," he said in an article in the *Baltimore Evening Sun* newspaper in 1932. During the game, a Maryland lineman rose up and yelled at some of the Yale players, "So this is Yale." It was enough to inspire the Elis to their come-from-behind charge in the second half.

A tie against rival Johns Hopkins in the last game of the season prevented Bryd from setting a record for most wins in a season.

Call Out the Band

In November 1923, the school's military department released a notice that announced the formation of a new school band, which would be a part of the ROTC program.

It mentioned the following inducements to those who signed up: two trips with the football team; a band leader from "one of the bands in Washington; "distinctive uniform" of white flannel pants and Maryland sweaters and caps; another uniform for military ceremonies; new instruments; free admission to athletic events and course credit. Thirty-two students attended the first practice.

Not Exactly Ship-Shape

When Burton Shipley gathered his first basketball team for practice in 1924, he didn't have much to work with. Most players had very little basketball experience; only two, including future longtime lacrosse coach Jack Faber, had played a good deal of basketball. The rest were athletes from other Maryland sports teams.

Nonetheless, Maryland won its first game 41-22 against George Washington University in the newly constructed Ritchie Coliseum, which opened in 1922.

Injuries and untimely illness contributed to a series of losses for Maryland, which ended its first regular season at 5-7. Maryland lost in the second round of the Southern Conference tournament

Meanwhile, its freshman team finished the year 12-1. The team scored 81 points in one game, considered quite an accomplishment since a center jump took place after each basket. Fraternities and sororities each had leagues, and the school strongly supported varsity games. Maryland basketball was firmly planted in the culture of Maryland State College.

The varsity hoopers responded with two decisively success-ful seasons. The 1924-25 team beat defending intercollegiate champion Columbia and ended the regular season 11-4. It lost in the second round of the conference tournament.

The 1925-26 team did even better, finishing 14-3, including a win over eventual conference champion North Carolina after UNC star "Dead Shot" Cobb missed a "snowbird" (an easy shot) late in the game, according to *The Diamondback*.

But Maryland struggled in the conference tournament, los-ing, surprisingly, in the first round to Mississippi A&M.

Is It Football or Basketball?

It helped that Maryland's basketball team included some members of the football team, because the action at times re-sembled a gridiron game. Basketball at that time did not have standardized rules, so players often intimidated opponents with physical play.

Faber recalls in *Maryland Basketball: Red, White and Amen*, "The man with the ball had the privilege of driving to the basket. If anybody got in his way it was just too bad.

Buddy Ensor, one of the players on Maryland's first official team, remembers splitting an ear in one game. Curley Byrd, sit-ting on the Maryland bench, arrived at a quick solution. He put a football helmet on Ensor and sent him back into the game.

Stickmen Make Immediate Impact

When the first officially recognized lacrosse season took place on campus in 1924, it had become one of the more popular and successful athletic activities on campus. Maryland had joined the Southern Division of the Intercollegiate Lacrosse League in 1923, along with such teams as Johns Hopkins, Lehigh and Penn, and was ranked third in the nation in 1922.

The Aggies won the Southern Division in 1925. Maryland also showed it could do well against international competition. In 1926, the lacrosse team beat a combined team from England's Cambridge and Oxford Universities, 11-4.

Maryland had four coaches in its first four seasons, but the changes didn't matter. From its first year in 1924 to 1943—before a two-year break in competition due to World War II—Maryland lacrosse had the most national success of any men's team on campus. Maryland was United States Intercollegiate Lacrosse Association champ three times (1936, 1939, and 1940) and co-champ once (1937). During that time, they sported a 136-25-2 record. All-American Bill Evans led the nation in scoring in 1929 with 37 goals.

R.V. Truitt was the first coach from 1924-27, followed by Jack Faber until 1930. Then Faber and Al Heagy were co-coaches until 1963. The two amassed an incredible 224-52-2 record, for an .809 winning percentage. They won eight of 10 ACC championships and contended during their time as coaches (the conference started play in 1954).

Early on, the lacrosse players received strong vocal support from their fans, perhaps too strong, said *The Diamondback* in 1924. Two weeks after a 5-3 win over rival Navy, an editorial in the paper chastised the Aggies fans for cheering such things as "sock him," "kill him," and "lay on the wood." The paper said the activity was against the rules of the lacrosse league and warned that the behavior could result in a forfeit.

Unstoppable Urso

No quest for a national lacrosse title matches the men's team's effort in 1973. Up to that time, Maryland had won six exclusive national titles and shared two others. Maryland dominated its opponents that season, outscoring nine teams 150-51 heading into the championship game against none other than Johns Hopkins. The closest margin of victory for the unbeaten Terps that season was a 9-4 win over Baltimore. Twice the Terps scored more than 20 goals, including 27 in the opening game against Duke.

By the time the championship game arrived, the Maryland and Hopkins had become perhaps the most contentious collegiate lacrosse rivalry in the country. The two teams could not even agree on who led the series.

Maryland claimed they had the advantage, 27-24-1. Hopkins countered with a 28-25-2 record in their favor. Hopkins counted four wins over the Terps prior to 1924, when Maryland first officially counted records. Maryland counted two wins over Hopkins in a summer league in 1943.

The two teams had played seven games since the national title contest in 1967, with the Terps winning three of them, including a 17-4 conquest about three weeks before the two met in

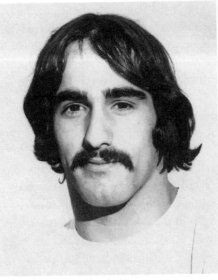

Frank Urso

the 1973 NCAA title match. In 1972, the Terps lost to Hopkins in the semifinal of the first NCAA tournament, 9-6, at Byrd Stadium.

The rivalry could not be much more intense by the time the two met in Philadelphia for the 1973 championship. Maryland was ranked number one, Hopkins number two. Tournament organizers picked Philadelphia because of its proximity between Long Island and Maryland, considered the top two breeding grounds for lacrosse in the U.S.

The game was played in historic Franklin Field on Astroturf, which Maryland had not played on in two years. To prepare, the Terps trained on an Astroturf field at Washington Redskins Park in Northern Virginia. And head coach Bud Beardmore bought 26 waffle-soled shoes to provide better traction on the surface than tennis shoes or cleats.

With memories of the earlier resounding defeat still vivid, Hopkins started the game with a stall, and it worked. Hopkins scored the first two goals and led 5-2 at halftime. Beardmore said Maryland expected Hopkins to play a stall, but not so early in the game. It took Maryland a half to adjust to the strategy.

"That was an unbelievably frustrating game," said midfielder Frank Urso, a freshman in that game. "We were not prepared at all for that style. We were run and gun, a freelance-style team. I remember at times sitting in the box next to the bench, waiting to go back in the game, yelling at the coach of their team about playing this kind of style. We had to mentally adjust."

Urso said the Terps had to put the ball in the hands of the right players. "We knew we would have the ball a lot in the second half, but we had to use better judgement." At halftime, Beardmore told Urso to take control of the game. "I was pleading to him to just give me the ball and he confirmed for me to take the ball," said Urso. "I don't think we ever felt we weren't going to win it. It was more to figure out how we were going to win it. We were unsuccessful at getting control, going ahead for a couple goals."

The Blue Jays controlled the game in all but the third period, and Maryland took advantage with four unanswered goals in the first five and a half minutes of that period. But Hopkins fought back and pulled ahead 9-7 with little more than 12 minutes remaining.

Lacrosse fans received a glimpse of the grand and immediate future of Maryland lacrosse when Urso scored arguably the two most important goals of his glorious career. The first was an extra-man goal to tie the game with 5:44 remaining. "We felt then that we were back and we were controlling the game," said Urso. The next goal, scored 10 yards from goal, came 5:18 into the overtime to clinch Maryland's first NCAA tournament title since it began in 1971.

"It was very congested," he said. "I remember seeing an opening to the goal. I couldn't see the keeper. I figured the keeper, Les Mathews, couldn't see me. It was just a matter of getting it on goal in that spot. I just needed to take a good shot." He did, planting the ball in the upper right corner.

"It was probably, from an excitement perspective, the most exciting goal of my career."

Urso ended the game with three goals and an assist. He says that 1973 championship team was unique.

"I've played on two U.S. teams," he said. "That probably was the best team I ever played on." Twelve Terps were named All-American that year, the most of any one Terp team.

Maryland lost to Hopkins, 17-12 in the 1974 NCAA title game, one of two Terp loses to the Blue Jays that season. But in

1975, Maryland beat Hopkins by eight goals during the regular season and again played in the NCAA title match, this time against Navy.

Navy had beaten the Terps by a goal earlier in the year, and the midshipmen got out to a 4-3 lead late in the first quarter.

Urso then took over. Commanded by Beardmore to "call his own number" and take control, Urso scored three goals in the next two minutes, putting the Terps ahead 6-5 by the end of the period.

Maryland used that momentum to take a 9-6 halftime lead. They led 14-11 early in the fourth period before scoring six of the game's last eight goals. The 20-goal total broke Hopkins' record of 17 in a title match. Urso's five goals were also a final game record.

"That was an odd season for us," he said. "We had a whole lot of talent, but didn't start the season off well." Maryland has not won a national title since Urso departed College Park, although they played in the NCAA tournament final four times after he graduated.

He Coulda Been a Football Player

Lacrosse was not the only sport Frank Urso wanted to play in college. He was recruited out of Brentwood High School in Long Island for his football talent as much for his lacrosse skills. Ohio State, Texas and Maryland all wanted Urso to play football for them, and for good reason.

Urso was a High School All-American as a running back for Brentwood. In eight years of playing football, Urso says he never lost a game. Urso won four state titles at Brentwood.

Beardmore, an assistant coach with Jerry Claiborne's Terps football team, recruited Urso to be a running back and a lacrosse player. Urso opted for Maryland because he initially wanted to play both sports in college, and the Terps offered the best combination of both.

But by the time football season arrived, Urso decided to focus just on lacrosse. "For whatever dumb reason, I decided not to play football," said Urso, who admits he still regrets not having played football in college. "There were some bad feelings from high school football, dumb stuff." Urso would not elaborate.

Urso ended his Maryland career with many accolades. He was the team's top point scorer his junior year. The Terps appeared in the NCAA tournament final each of his four years. He was voted the nation's outstanding midfielder in 1974 and 1976 and was the only Terp voted to the NCAA tournament 25th anniversary team in 1996. He is the only Maryland player to have his number retired.

The Green Bay Packers invited Urso to try out for the team after his lacrosse career at Maryland ended. He decided against it, instead helping to build a professional indoor lacrosse league, which he had been helping promote since he was a Terp freshman.

The league promised to make Urso its highest-paid player, around $50,000 a year plus a percentage of the revenue from attendance.

Three weeks after turning down the Packers, Urso received a call from a reporter at *The Washington Post*, who asked if he could talk to Urso. When the reporter stressed immediacy, Urso asked why. The reporter wanted Urso to comment on the news that the box lacrosse league was folding.

He said he was so shocked at the news he declined comment to the reporter. With no athletic pursuits available, Urso opened a bar in Washington called One Flight Up. He played lacrosse sporadically and one year coached the McGarvey's Saloon lacrosse team in Annapolis. He now lives in Boothwin, Pennsylvania, and works as a regional manager for Circuit City.

Getting On Track

In its early days, around the early 1920s, cross-country at Maryland was referred to in the yearbook as "the suicide club." No explanation was given, but it appears to be a reference to the sadistic nature of the sport.

Cross-country was started primarily because enough students felt the school needed more sports.

Byrd and others, *The Diamondback* reported, decided to give "those students desirous of good, clean body-developing exercise an opportunity to get it as well as make a team that would uphold Maryland's athletic traditions."

In 1921, 38 men showed up for the fist day of practice. After three weeks of walking and jogging, 23 of them dropped out. Nine runners were ultimately picked for the team.

There were mixed results that year. They team came within one point of defeating Washington and Lee, the champions of the South Atlantic. But they lost a dual meet to Virginia, placing just three runners in the top 10. The team's top runner, described only as Compher by *The Diamondback*, stopped running halfway through the course.

"When the short training of the Maryland men and poor facilities for the sport are considered, the showing made on Saturday seems creditable," wrote *The Diamondback*.

The relative success of the team did not please the student newspaper. It called the effort "deplorable," a "seeming lack of spirit not only on the part of those who dropped out of the sport but of those who did not even try for the team when it was organized." The paper called for those qualified to compete in the sport to do so.

In 1924, the team beat only one other team, the Aloysius Club of Washington, to win the South Atlantic Championship. Maryland runners finished fourth through 13th. Individual runners from many other schools also competed.

In 1926, interest in the sport increased when "major" letters were awarded in the sport.

Share a Beer with That Man

By 1914, interest in track and field had grown strong enough to hold an annual intercollegiate meet on campus. Some 300 contestants competed in the event, the fourth year the meet was held. It was the largest track competition in the South.

Track at M.A.C. was progressing nicely until World War I cancelled many meets during the 1917 outdoor season, including the South Atlantic championships.

Maryland's men's track team endured a slump during and for a few years after World War I. The 1925 yearbook, *Tarra Mariae*, reports the indoor team "competed with honors" three years after it was "reconstructed" at some of the best meets in the district. The team trained indoors on a small gym track, which apparently helped them more effectively navigate the right-angled turns on some of the tracks on which they competed. Maryland won the South Atlantic AAU championships in 1922 and 1923 and started fall training for the first time in 1923.

That year, a student with the last name Beers is listed as Maryland's first official champion after winning the Southern Conference Championship shot put. He also won the event in 1924.

Renovations to Byrd Stadium in the late 1920s forced the track team to train at Eastern High School, Catholic University and Western High.

Frosh Have Found Their Place

Each sport at Maryland included a freshman team by 1925. Before then, only the baseball and football programs featured frosh squads. Difficulty in finding a place for the freshman teams to practice and dress on campus forced a delay in the dawning of the teams. Still, the school yearbook says the first-year teams were assigned the campus "gullys and hillsides" to practice.

Conference Call

Maryland's men's track and field athletes showed more varied proficiency in the 1930s. In 1934, sophomore Earl Widmyer, nicknamed the "Hagerstown Flier," won the school's first Southern Conference 100-meter title, and he set the school record of 9.8 seconds while winning the conference title the next year. He also won the conference 220-yard title in 1935 and indoor 60-yard titles from 1933 to 1935

Maryland won the 440-yard dash in 1935 (Bob Archer) and 1936 (George Cronin), both in 49.6 seconds. Cronin also won the pole vault in 1938. Coleman Headley won conference titles in 1936 (one mile) and 1938 (880).

1935 was a breakout year for men's track at Maryland. That year it finished second in the conference to North Carolina. From 1938 to 1941, the team finished no worse than third in the conference standings.

Indoors, Maryland won the indoor 440-yard run from 1935 to 1940, with three runners—Warren Evena, Frank Cronin and Al Miller—each winning twice. It also won the mile relay from 1934-1940.

The outdoor tracksters won the conference crown from 1951 to 1953. That year Maryland track broke from the conference to join the Atlantic Coast Conference, and track would dominate conference competition like no other in Maryland history.

A Victory Worthy of Poetry

In 1926, Maryland football achieved further national acclaim when it returned to the Yale Bowl to beat the Elis 15-0. Yale approached the game with a touch of indifference. They started the game with reserves on the field while its coach, Tad Jones, sat in the stands. *The Baltimore Sun* published the following poem to honor the victory:
"When the boys are in a panic,
Dreading foes that loom titanic,
Note the man who grows satanic,
Shouts 'absurd.'
This gent loves to find 'em burley,
Brainy, brawny, sour and surly,
You can't reckon with Curley;
He's a Byrd."

In Fits About Snitz

One of the more colorful characters on the 1926 football team was running back Gerald (Snitz) Snyder, who helped popularize the fake reverse and who became the second Maryland player to be named to the Associated Press All-American team.

Snyder came to Maryland from the Pennsylvania coalmine area with a rugged approach to the game and an apathy for academics. Against Navy his freshman year, he was ineligible due to poor grades. With a substitute freshman coach looking the other way, he put on another player's uniform and played during the second half. He says with a laugh that they never knew.

Snyder says he was the reason Byrd decided to change the way the team's captains were picked. Snyder was one of few seniors in 1928 and was expected to be named captain. But Byrd had suspended Snyder at least one time for inappropriate off-field behavior.

Team members had picked the captains. But Byrd said the captaincy had turned into a competition for fraternities to elect a yearlong leader. In his book, *Kings of American Football*, author Bealle called it "political football." Byrd opted for game captains instead, a system that lasted 15 years.

Largest Margin of Victory

In 1927, Maryland started the season in a way it never had before or has since, with an 80-0 win over Washington College. It still is the most points scored in one game by the Maryland football team. Still, Maryland finished 4-7 that season, with losses to Yale, in front of 32,000 fans, and Hopkins, watched by 18,000 spectators. That season, Maryland ventured further south than it had before, with loses to Florida and Vanderbilt.

Maryland finished the next season 6-3-1, with wins over Yale and Johns Hopkins. After the win over Yale, some felt the Elis would soon stop playing such a small school as Maryland, especially after a loss. The teams played for the last time in 1930. Yale won the last duel, 40-13.

For Bosey, Any Ball Will Do

Following a frustrating year plagued by injury, the 1927-28 basketball team rebounded well. They finished 14-4 overall, 8-1 in the conference. But the Aggies did not play in the conference tournament.

The yearbook blamed "unfortunate scheduling." Coach Shipley simply said "[The school] told us we weren't going." First-year player Al Heagy, later a longtime Maryland lacrosse coach with Jack Faber, said "I believe it had something to do with finances."

Misfortune—illness and again injury—hurt the team the following season, which ended with its first losing record. But there was hope on the horizon, in the name of Louis "Bosey" Berger, who led the unbeaten freshman team by scoring 101 points in nine games. The play of Berger, also a member of the football and baseball teams, was the appetizer for a delicious main course of Maryland championship basketball that was soon to come.

Berger's Big Appetite for Athletics

The Yale and Maryland football teams played to a 13-13 tie in 1929, but if it had not been for Berger, Maryland could easily have lost the game. Berger first entered the game in the second half after Maryland's two starting halfbacks had been injured. Maryland was down, 13-0.

Up to that point in the season, Berger saw action in only play as an end, and he suffered an injury. He did not expect to play in the Yale game and viewed the trip as a sightseeing adventure. He was surprised when Byrd said he would play the second half. Berger caught three passes in the game, two for touchdowns.

Berger was also good enough in baseball to play six years for three teams in major league baseball. The Bosey Berger Award has been given annually since 1935 to Maryland's top senior player. And Coach Byrd said he could have made Burger into a 49-second quarter-miler.

Free Meal Makes Berger a Football Player

Berger did not play football at McKinley Tech High School in Baltimore, concentrating instead on baseball and basketball. He had hoped for a scholarship at Duke, but the Blue Devils never offered him one. Berger then opted to attend Maryland, where early on he lived with former Maryland quarterback and, at the time, baseball coach Burton Shipley. Assistant football coach Jack Faber told Berger that he would get a free late meal if he played football. A big eater, the aptly named Berger could not ignore that opportunity.

By the time Berger left Maryland in 1932 he was a two-time All-American in basketball and an honorable mention All-American in football. He was also vice president of the student body and was selected the school's model citizen.

And he had fun with athletics. "He was real likeable," said Harry Hess, the basketball manager from 1929 to 1931, in the book *Maryland Basketball: Red, White and Amen.* "He horsed around a little bit and kept the spirits up. He was not swell-headed at all, a fun guy and a picture athlete."

Berger was Maryland's first All-American basketball player, in 1931 and 1932. He was the only Maryland basketball All-American in the first half of the 20th century.

Pigeons and Pampering Keep Tandem Prepared

Berger teamed with back Shorty Chalmers to form one of the most dangerous pass-catch combinations in Maryland history, despite the fact Chalmers lined up out on the wing in the double-wing formation. Berger patrolled the other wing.

They also worked well together on the baseball team. Both were infielders. Chalmers, who stood only five feet, eight inches, had a penchant for pigeons. He kept some in his top dresser drawer at school and admittedly exercised them in front of a mirror every morning. Some of his teammates helped him catch the birds. Chalmers later raised pigeons, at one time boasting a stable of 110.

Chalmers's roommate, running back Ray Poppelman, slept on perhaps the most famous bed in Maryland athletic history. To secure Poppelman's interest in attending Maryland, Byrd agreed to give Chalmers a special bed. Poppelman was unhappy with the bunk beds the school provided.

Adding Some Punch to Byrd's Best Team, Poppelman and Woods Lead the Old Line

Poppelman and linebacker/blocking back Al "Punchy" Woods were playing for the Marine Corps team that occasionally scrimmaged Maryland. Byrd recruited Poppelman and Woods after watching them in those workouts. The two earned the first full scholarships given to a Maryland athlete.

Woods had a reputation as a tough player. He would hit players head on, forcing him to occasionally black out. At a game against VMI, a referee so infuriated Woods that he chased him into the stands. Faber had to pull Woods off of the referee.

Berger, Chalmers, Poppelman and Woods were the nucleus of Byrd's most successful team in 1931. Woods and Chalmers scored touchdowns in a season-opening 13-0 win over Washington College, despite nine Maryland fumbles. Chalmers threw the winning touchdown in the 6-0 win over Navy. In front of 16,000 fans at Griffith Stadium. Poppelman scored three touchdowns and his running set up two others against VMI. He ran for 156 yards and two touchdowns in a win over Virginia Tech.

School Not Bowled Over by Success

That win prompted talk of the school's first ever postseason bowl appearance as Maryland prepared for its next contest over Vanderbilt. An editorial in the student newspaper quelled that enthusiasm. It said Maryland had a policy against playing games after the regular season. "There is such a thing as tradition and an athletic policy which is not jelly-like in substance," it said. "Football at Maryland never has entered the commercial world ... the game will never deteriorate into a sheer money-making spectacle."

A 39-12 loss against Vanderbilt muted any further discussion about a bowl game that season and ended Maryland's chances for a Southern Conference title.

During wins in Maryland's next two games, Poppelman rushed for 330 yards. And he scored three times and rushed for 201 yards in the last game of the season, a 41-6 win over Western Maryland, in what was considered the last significant win of Byrd's football coaching career at Maryland.

Maryland was not penalized once in the game. The team amassed 441 yards to Western Maryland's 203 yards. Even Woods, known for his blocking, rushed for 72 yards.

Byrd considered only his 1923 team as talented as the 1931 team. The Aggies finished 8-1-1 and 4-0 in the Southern Conference. Poppelman compiled 1350 yards that season, topping Snyder's record of 1255.

Conference Contenders:
Basketball Claims
First Conference Title

The football team was not the only Maryland sports team to contend for the Southern Conference title in 1931. Maryland basketball won its first conference title that year.

The men's basketball team had turned things around the previous season, winning 16 games and losing six. But they lost again in the first round of the conference tournament, this time to Kentucky.

The Terrapins won the conference title despite some solid obstacles. After the team's leading scorer from the previous year, Bob Gaylor, quit school, they had a roster of just eight players.

But it was a solid eight, including the crew from the undefeated freshman team of the 1928-29 season.

One of those players, adept outside shooter Ed Ronkin, helped Maryland win a pivotal game over North Carolina at home. He scored the tying basket in regulation and added two more points in overtime to give the Aggies the lead for good in the 33-31 victory.

When Ronkin returned to his room following a late night savoring the win, he discovered he was locked out of his room. He had to climb through a window to get to bed. Shipley told him the next day that he had lost his starting job and that he had to learn to come back on time.

Naturally Up

Shipley said the strongest characteristic of that championship team was confidence.

"We just did everything naturally then," Shipley said in *Maryland Basketball: Red, White and Amen.* "We never mentioned that 'get up for the game' stuff. I thought it was up all the time."

The Aggies, seeded second in the conference tournament, were psyched for their opening game in Atlanta and beat LSU, 37-33. In its next game against North Carolina, Maryland fell behind 13-1, but held the Tar Heels to one second-half point and won 19-17. Berger made the game winner, but the Terps missed often that day. Their field goal percentage was only .094.

Berger converted a free throw that clinched a 26-25 semifinal win over Georgia, but he saved his best for last in the championship game against Kentucky.

Using an offensive scheme that stressed setting picks and cutting to the basket, Maryland led 18-7 at the half. But Kentucky took a two-point lead with two minutes remaining, signaled by the timekeeper raising his gun in the air. Ronkin then fed Berger for a basket to tie the game. After Maryland rebounded a missed Kentucky free throw, Ronkin and Berger teamed up again. Berger's layup won the game for Maryland.

Ronkin secured the win by stealing the next tap from the center circle, and after Berger missed a shot that would have been icing on the cake, both teams fell on the floor from exhaustion.

Improved shooting certainly helped Maryland win the game. They were 12 of 31 from the field, or .419 percent.

Of Berger, the *Atlanta Journal* wrote: "Louis Berger was born with blood of ice and nerves of steel and the old heart and brains that could keep functioning when other around him were twittering with dismay."

A special committee met the team at Union Station in Washington, D.C. and later escorted the players before the student body in the gym. It's unknown how late Ronkin stayed out that night.

Happy Tunes for the Hoopers

For the 1931-32 season, Shipley faced a dilemma that every coach would like to have—too many good players. He returned all his starters and had available another strong crop of young players from the previous year's freshman team who claimed they could beat the older guys any time.

Maryland lost its first two games, but then won 14 in a row, including a game against Navy in the newly opened Ritchie Coliseum and every other game played at the new arena that season. The new building, named after then governer Albert Ritchie, seated up to 5,000 spectators and cost $200,000 to build. The crowd against Navy was the largest to attend a basketball game in the South Atlantic region.

Maryland had plenty of good times that season, punctuated by the harmonies and jocularity of team clown Spencer "Spidey" Chase, a lanky forward. Chase was known to sing to himself while he played.

Time Was Not on Their Side

Maryland also played some sour tunes during the 1931-32 season. Curley Byrd claims victory was stolen from Maryland that year in its season opener at Wisconsin when the clock operator let time run beyond regulation. With the lead, Maryland was trying to run out the clock, but Jack Norris attempted to score and missed. Wisconsin sent the game into overtime and went on to win by two points.

Byrd said Wisconsin officials did not let the timer, a former professor at Maryland, shoot the gun to end the game when it was over.

The end to Maryland's season was equally as disturbing. For the first time, Maryland had finished first in the conference standings at the end of regulation season. The Aggies were primed to defend the conference tournament title.

But Berger and Ronkin fouled out early in the second half in the tournament's first game against Florida, and the Gators handed Maryland a stinging defeat, 39-24.

King Kong Keller

By the start of the next season, Maryland was part of a re- vised Southern Conference. All but 10 teams fled to the new Southeastern Conference.

Maryland fashioned winning seasons the next two years, but each time lost in the first round of the conference tournament, which was moved to Raleigh, North Carolina. They endured their second losing season under Shipley during the 1934-35 season, despite having three players whom Shipley placed on his all-time team: Vic Willis, Charlie Keller and Bill Guckeyson.

Keller was one of the best athletes to come out of Maryland. Keller was given the nickname King Kong for his stocky build, long arms and bushy hair. And he played basketball with a gorilla's abandon. Keller would do almost anything to get hold of the ball. Basketball coach Shipley said Keller wanted the ball more than anyone he ever coached.

But Keller was best at baseball. During the 1935 season, Keller batted .551 in his first 17 games. He ended his two-year baseball career with a .497 average, the best in Maryland history.

His baseball prowess prompted many major league scouts to travel to College Park and watch him play. He last played for Maryland in 1936 and signed with the New York Yankees while still a student at Maryland. Keller played in the 1939 World Se- ries for the Yankees against Cincinnati.

Maryland opted to not travel to the conference tournament at the end of the 1934-35 season. The conference opener was scheduled to take place the same day as the All-University night celebration.

Back to the Finals

Maryland basketball returned to the Southern Conference finals during the 1938-39 season for the first time in eight years.

Along the way, they endured one of the earliest challenges on Tobacco Road, the famed and feared corridor of North Carolina basketball schools that still pesters the Terps today.

In a four-day period that season, Maryland beat Duke and North Carolina, but lost to North Carolina State in overtime. Junior guard George Knepley, considered the best guard in the South that year, said of the State game in the book *Maryland Basketball: Red, White and Amen*, "The home coach picked his own officials, and you always had to whip a team by 10 points or you were a loser."

The Terps later gained revenge against NC State, beating them in the tournament semifinal by 24 points. But Clemson won the conference title by beating Maryland 39-27 in the final.

The next season, Maryland advanced to the semifinals of the conference tournament. But starting with the 1940-41 season, preparations for World War II (notably the Selective Service Act) depleted the school of high-quality athletes. For six years, Maryland baseball endured losing seasons, winning just one game in 1940-41.

6

Rifle Ladies Claim
First National Title

Maryland's Athletic Association officially recognized the women's rifle team in 1927, one year after they won the National Rifle Association's Intercollegiate Rifle Championships. The team was the first to win a national title at Maryland.

The women started competing in rifle in 1923. They never saw many of their competitors that year. Since most of the teams they faced were beyond travel limitations, results of many matches were sent by mail. That season the women's team received a challenge to shoot against St. Ann's Diocesan College of Natal, British South Africa. The "foreign shoot" took place on January 19. It took about a month before results reached each school after they were sent by mail. To personalize the competition, the Maryland women asked that the teams exchange pictures along with the results.

The School of Accurate Knox

Irene Knox said it was her eyesight that made her such a remarkable rifle shooter. Her coach, Sergeant Earl Henricks of the U.S. Army, Maryland's rifle instructor, said it was her hair color. Henricks said blondes make the best bull's-eye borers.

Knox, described by the *Washington Star* newspaper as "full o' pep and quite restless, a vivacious blonde," credited her far-sighted right eye for helping her locate the target with such remarkable accuracy.

Whatever the reason, there was no debating her talent. In winning the 1932 National Rifle Association's Women's Individual Intercollegiate Championship, Knox hit the bull's eye with 119 of 120 shots to earn 599 out of a possible 600 points. Knox, who had less than two years experience in target shooting, broke the women's record by four points and the men's record by two.

Knox capped her collegiate career by competing in the 1932 Summer Olympics.

The following poem was presented to Knox at a banquet during her reign of renowned rifle shooting:

In these dangerous days around D.C.
We must be very careful, you see
A certain young miss from Md. U.
Is a pretty good shot—she might aim at you.

Heavy Hitters

The boxing team, coached by William Whipp, lost all three of its matches during its first year in 1931. But that span of futility was short lived.

Stewart McCaw, also known as "the fighting Irishman," won the 1934 and 1935 Southern Conference title in the 175-pound weight class. In 1935, sophomore Ivan Nedomatsky won the 135-pound title despite breaking his hand in the bout.

Maryland picked a good time to host the Southern Conference championships in Ritchie Coliseum in 1937. That season, the Terps were undefeated in dual meets and won the Conference title. Ben Alperstein (135 pounds) and Tom Birmingham (125 pounds) were conference champs and competed in the National Intercollegiate Championships in Sacramento, California. Alpersetein brought home the lightweight crown; Nedomatsky also won a conference title.

Wins by Alperstein, Frank Cronin and New Cox helped Maryland win its second Southern Conference title in 1939.

Baltimore's Boxing Brothers

Benny Alperstein was the first male athlete to win an individual national championship at Maryland. He and his younger brother, Hotsy, typified the successes achieved and hardships endured by Maryland boxers at that time.

When Benny Alperstein accepted a boxing scholarship at Maryland State College in 1935, boxing was in his blood. He says he started using his fists when he was old enough to walk, to defend himself out of necessity.

The Alperstein family of seven boys and one girl grew up near a boxing arena in the Italian neighborhood of Carlin Park in North Baltimore. As Jews, the Alpersteins were subject to constant mistreatment by many of the Christians in the neighborhood.

"We couldn't walk to school without a fight," said Benny Alperstein. "If you were Jewish, you were subject to beatings."

Benny's younger brother, Hotsy, was a boxing champion at Maryland in the early 1940s. "When I was going to Hebrew School, every night they were waiting for us to come down the steps, looking for a fight," he said. "We never backed away from anything."

And they had plenty of boys to fight. One family had 11 boys, another had nine. "All were professional fighters," said Hotsy Alperstein.

Harold "Red" Burman, whom the Alpersteins say fought Joe Louis for the heavyweight championship in 1936, lived across the street from the Alpersteins.

Benny joined the National Guard in Baltimore after high school to box in their tournaments. He was also enticed by the training table given to the boxers after the bouts and the $13-a-month pay.

Wisconsin Woes

Benny Alperstein first used boxing gloves when he fought for the National Guard, but he didn't receive any coaching. That came when he entered Maryland. Benny was offered a scholarship of room and board by his fraternity at Maryland as long as he waited on tables.

His coach at Maryland, Colonel Harvey Miller, was also the chairman of the D.C. Boxing Commission. Miller would bring in local professional boxers to train with the Maryland team during workouts in the basement rooms of Ritchie Coliseum.

"You learned a great deal from those guys," said Benny.

That environment helped shape the most dangerous brother boxing duo in the history of Maryland athletics. Benny was the first male athlete at Maryland to win a national intercollegiate title in an individual event.

Benny, who won national titles in 1937 and 1938, says he should have been a three-time national champ, but he lost to a fighter from the University of Wisconsin at the national tournament in 1939 in Wisconsin.

"Dr. Charley Mackert [a physical education professor at Maryland] told me not to go because I couldn't win out there," said Benny. "I said, I've got to go."

One year, Tom Birmingham, a featherweight, also went to the national collegiate championships with Benny. But a weakness for a heavy soft beverage combined with a slight weight problem hurt his chances of winning a national title.

"He had to lose a couple of pounds out there, and after he lost them he had a yen for a milkshake," said Benny. Following an afternoon weigh-in, before Birmingham's first bout of the tournament later that evening, he couldn't resist the drink.

"I said, you've got to fight tonight, what the hell you going to drink a milkshake for? It was the biggest mistake. He got hit in the stomach and he felt it coming up. I was in his corner. He was able to hold it in, but it affected his boxing." Birmingham lost the bout.

One Lightning Strike Too Many

Hotsy says he earned a full scholarship to Maryland on Benny's reputation.

"He told [athletic director] Geary Eppley that he had a kid brother who can fight as good as him but if you don't give him a scholarship real quick, he's gonna go to another school," said Hotsy, who entered Maryland in 1938.

Hotsy was the only fighter on the freshman team to win a bout. In fact, he won them all. Hotsy never fought for a national title, claiming the school didn't want to pay to send him. But he was a finalist in the Eastern Intercollegiate championships and the Southern Conference championships.

Hotsy Alperstein fought the Southern Conference title bout his junior season with a broken jaw after receiving a head-butt to the left side of his face in the quarterfinal bout.

"I couldn't open my jaw, couldn't eat anything," he said. "I wasn't about to tell the coach; he would have pulled me out of there."

He managed to avoid getting hit in the face through the semi-final bout and up to the final 20 seconds of the final bout.

"It was an even fight," said Hotsy. "Then he hit me right on that spot, and I went down and came right back up, and that was enough to win a split decision. It was like a shot of lightning hit me in the head."

The Cons of Fighting Pros

The Alpersteins say boxing was bigger than any other sport on campus in the 1930s. Bouts, often held after basketball games, commonly drew up to 6,000 spectators at Ritchie Coliseum. Most of the crowd, say the Alpersteins, showed up for the boxing matches.

"You couldn't get in Ritchie," said Hotsy. "They would line up the night before the bouts."

The Alpersteins said boxing was so strong then because many professionals fought in college to get an education. Most, they say, never went to high school.

They said many pro boxers would change their name in college to hide evidence of their professional history. They often attended a college far from their hometown to make it easier to hide their identity.

"Catholic must have had a slew of pros on their team," said Hotsy. "Those guys were so good. We were great enemies with Catholic. We were taught to hate each other."

Hotsy fought his first varsity bout at Catholic. Thousands of fans, most of them unfriendly to the Maryland boxers, crowded into Catholic's gymnasium. Hotsy remembers vividly the unpleasant sounds he heard during the walk from the locker room to the ring.

"All I heard was 'Kill that Jew, kill that Jew,' and I started smiling," said Hotsy. "My coach, Harvey Miller, said, 'What the hell are you smiling about? I'm ready to pull the whole team out of here.' I said, 'Coach, it reminds me of my old neighborhood. I don't care how good this guy is, he ain't gonna win.' I don't remember many names, but that guy's name was Huck Hughes. I beat him three years in a row."

No-Knock-Out Hotsy

The brothers had different styles in the ring. "Benny would knock out his opponents. I would never try to knock them out," said Hotsy. "I always felt sorry for the guy, they've got their families there, their relatives there, their classmates there. Why would you embarrass they guy? I'd win on points. I knew within one minute in the ring whether I could beat the guy or not."

Hotsy stuck true to his style throughout his college career, except for his last regular-season bout in a Maryland uniform. His coach, Bobby Goldstein, told Hotsy he wanted him to knock out a North Carolina State opponent.

"He said you can't go four years and not knock somebody out," said Hotsy. "I said I didn't want to knock him out. The kid was so scared you could hear his heart beat from across the ring. He said, 'Hotsy, you'd be doing him a favor.' So I knocked him out in 33 seconds, and let me tell you something, I didn't sleep for two weeks. I felt so bad for doing that. He shouldn't have been in there."

Byrd Flies Away

When Byrd was promoted to vice president of the school in 1932, much of his attention shifted to developing areas of the school other than athletics. He also still was a sports writer for *The Washington Star* and had interests in a bank, a publishing company and a real estate company. Byrd relied more on his assistant coaches for two years, and Maryland suffered two successive losing seasons. It also did not help that Maryland lost eight starters from the 1931 team.

In 1933, Byrd relinquished his job as head football coach, although he would not officially leave the team until two years later. He was one of five named to a coaching board that managed the football team.

In 1934 Faber, the Maryland quarterback in 1924 and 1925, stepped in as the acting head coach, as what he called "a front" for Byrd, who coached the team on game days and most practices. They managed one of Maryland's better teams that year, finishing 7-3.

When Faber took the position permanently in 1935, he was also the varsity lacrosse coach, freshman basketball coach, freshman football coach and instructor in bacteriology. So Byrd decided to hire Frank Dobson as the football field coach. Faber served as liaison between Dobson and Byrd. Faber said he was happy with the arrangement.

The Many Athletic Gifts of Bill Guckeyson

The year 1934 was also known for the emergence of Bill Guckeyson as a football player. Byrd called him the best player in Maryland history.

Guckeyson was the son of circus performers, and he played football with an acrobatic flair. The Maryland native did not play organized football until entering Maryland. He departed the school a two-time All-Southern Conference halfback.

Guckeyson's athletic accomplishments extended beyond the football field. He won two letters in basketball, one in baseball, two in track and three in football. He threw the javelin 208 feet, five inches, nearly made the 1936 Olympic team, and won the Southern Conference javelin title in 1935. He also did well throwing the shot put and the discus. In six dual meets in his senior year at Maryland, Guckeyson scored 83 of the team's 90 points.

Jim Kehoe, a Maryland track star and later athletic director at Maryland, called Guckeyson the best all-around athlete he ever saw.

Said Faber of Guckeyson, in the book, *The Terrapins: Maryland Football*, "He was a fine passer, a sure-handed receiver, a sufficient blocker, and a demon defensive player. He could do anything. He was quick and fast. No one taught him how to play. He was too good to coach."

And almost seemed too good to be true. Guckeyson was quiet and did not drink, swear, or smoke. His exploits in 1935 highlighted his football career at Maryland.

Guckeyson ran four times for 100 yards and one touchdown and punted seven times with a 57-yard average in a win over St. John's; punted 13 times with a 47-yard average and scored the only touchdown in a win over VPI; had a 75-yard quick kick, an 80-yard punt, passed for a touchdown, and his runs set up two others in a win over Florida; ran 50 yards for a touchdown and 90 yards on a kickoff off return for another score in a win over Georgetown. Maryland finished the season 7-2-2.

Guckeyson missed the first three games of the 1936 season due to injury, and Maryland finished 6-5-0. Still, first-year coach Frank Dobson had a firm understanding of Guckeyson's football legacy.

Dobson coached football for four decades, from, as he said in *The Terrapins: Maryland Football,* "the University of Georgia to the University of Maryland." Guckeyson, he said, was the best athlete he had ever known.

Guckeyson later became a war pilot. He was shot down and killed in Europe in 1944 while on a bombing mission during World War II.

His legacy at Maryland lives in many ways, perhaps most demonstrably in the annual Bill Guckeyson award the M-Club hands out at its annual awards banquet. First presented in 1958, it is given to a two-sport athlete who has lettered for two years.

8

Fields Finds Glory

As early as when he was a sophomore in high school in 1933, Tom Fields often walked a half mile to Route 1, a highway near his Hyasttsville, Maryland home, and hitchhiked two miles to the University of Maryland. Once there, he'd crawl through some broken windows into a dirty and muddy area under the old Byrd Stadium near fraternity row and change into his running clothes. The assertive youngster then would start running on the nearby track, where the University of Maryland track team was working out.

"The first couple of times I went up there, I hadn't been invited there," said Fields. "I just hopped out on the track and ran a mile. Then I'd walk around a bit and run two miles. They didn't know who I was." Soon enough, the Maryland runners noticed Fields. "Some of the athletes jogged up to me and said, 'Hey kid, what are you doing? You're going to kill yourself.' One of those was Jim Kehoe, who had been at Maryland for one year.

"I remember well," said Kehoe. "He was very tenacious, very determined, very ambitious."

Fields added youthful energy to an already established track and field program at Maryland. Fields says the team "kind of adopted me. I went to all their meets, and I can remember sitting with the girlfriend of the conference half-mile champion, Coleman Headley, while he was running."

Not surprisingly, Tom Fields had left an impression at Maryland even before he completed his first lap as a runner at the school in 1937.

Fields's charm and affable personality pervaded his four years at Maryland, a time that made him Maryland's first All-American in cross-country and one of the top track distance runners in the program's history. He was a four-time conference champion in the two-mile (three indoor, one outdoor).

Some 30 years later, Fields started serving as the executive director of the Maryland Educational Foundation, which raised money to pay for scholarships for student athletes. In that role, Fields helped develop a financial base for the program that thrives today.

No Wrong-Way Fields

Fields's running career at Maryland is filled with tales of adventure and misstep that mostly led to some form of success. While a member of the freshman cross-country team, he traveled to Charlottesville for a meet against the University of Virginia.

"When they took us out there to see the course, I didn't pay much attention," he said. "I was a little confused when I come up to a dead end. I could go left or right. So I sat there, threw rocks for a while until a Virginia runner caught up, and I said, 'Which way?' He said, 'That way,' and off I took."

Fields won that race and every other one in which he competed as a freshman.

As a sophomore, Fields and his teammates on the varsity experienced another adventure in Charlottesville. When Maryland arrived, they faced two surprises. The course had changed, and they faced a transfer student from the University of Michigan whom no one from Maryland knew about.

After running up "a horrible mountain," as Fields described it, he descended the hill behind the runner from Michigan. "I came out of the hill with a burst of speed," said Fields. "As I ran by the guy from Michigan State, I smiled. Almost killed me to hold my breath that long, but he folded right there."

Fields hit the tape together with teammates Jim Kehoe and Mason Chronister, leading Maryland to the victory.

The Penn Relays

His junior year, Fields and teammates Allie Miller, Kehoe and Chronister did something at the prestigious Penn Relays that has not since been matched by any Maryland distance runners. Maryland won the three Championship of America distance relays at the meet—the distance medley relay, the four-mile relay and the two-mile relay.

On Saturday, Fields gave Maryland a 60-yard lead after his leadoff leg of the four-mile relay. Bobby Condon, Kehoe and Chronister completed the victory.

Later that day, Fields sat out the two-mile relay. He witnessed one of the most exciting races of the day. Kehoe battled a runner from New York University for the lead down the entire backstretch of their anchor leg, and ended up winning by an inch.

The prize for winners of Penn Relays Championship of America competitions is a gold watch. "You talk about getting high on drugs, there was no way we could be any higher than we were that in that meet," said Fields. "To be in the Penn Relays, running for those gold watches, your knees almost hit you in the chin when they came up. They were the first watches I'd ever owned other than the one I got at a pawn shop for five dollars."

Grinding It Out in the Garden

One of the fondest memories of Fields's senior season came while running a one-mile anchor leg of a relay race at a meet in Madison Square Garden in New York City.

Fields received the baton 15 yards behind the leader, Campbell Kane of Indiana, a Big Ten champion in the mile and the 880. With three laps to go, he gave Kane an elbow as he slid by him on a turn,

"The crowd went crazy," said Fields. "Eighteen thousand people went mad. I knew if he caught me, he'd kill me. On the last lap, as we came into the home stretch, I'm in front, and I start easing to the right. I was going to run him up into the type-writers if I could.

"I broke the tape, but they said he won the race. He was one of the best in America. I had run my heart out."

Fields said he was sitting on the edge of the track, "recuperating" from the race, when Campbell walked by.

"He's all dressed up, already showered, and he's got a chorus girl on his arm," said Fields. "He's heading out, and he said, 'I'll see you in Baltimore next week, Tommy.'"

They never ran that week, but Fields says two other times he raced Campbell, he beat him, including at the NCAA cross-country championships the previous fall.

Guests of Honor and Heavy Tippers

Travels provided adventures aplenty for Fields and his running mates. Like most non-revenue sports teams of the time at Maryland, the keyword for travel was frugality. Fields, along with Kehoe, Chronister and Miller, wanted to run in a competitive meet to prepare for the upcoming Penn Relays.

"We went and saw our coach and told him we'd like to go down and run the Florida Relays, and he said that's great, but we don't have any money," said Fields.

The resourceful Fields would not be swayed. He convinced his uncle to take a week off and drive the four runners down to Florida and back, in a new Pontiac automobile. Fields then called a fraternity house at the school, and they agreed to let the runners stay there. To ease the trip, the track coach at the University of South Carolina agreed to set up sleeping arrangements for them as they drove down and back. "We stayed in the track dressing room and slept on army cots," said Fields.

At the meet, Fields, Kehoe and Chronister hit the tape together and won the mile. Later, Miller joined the trio to win the two-mile and one-mile relays.

"It got us ready for the Penn Relays," said Fields.

It also made them temporary heroes in Gainesville. When the runners returned to the fraternity house, they proudly placed their trophies on top of a baby grand piano. This so impressed the fraternity brothers that they invited the four runners to attend a dinner and dance later that night as honored guests.

Fields, ever the prankster, did not forget about the deed provided by his uncle. "We put my uncle on the spot," he said. "They're saying how great the Maryland guys were. We said, well, we owe it all to Coach Mac. He's our coach and he did it all. He wasn't a coach, he was an accountant. But he got up there and thanked them. It was a great experience."

So was winning the indoor two-mile relay at the Millrose Games in New York that same year. After returning to their hotel, they ran into coach Geary Eppley in the lobby.

"He says, 'Guys, you did great tonight,'" said Fields. "Get dressed, put your neckties on, come down to the main dining room, and have a good meal, then get a good night's sleep, I'll meet you here in the lobby, 10 o'clock tomorrow morning, and we'll go back to College Park.

"With that, he handed me a $10 bill to pay for dinner at the New Yorker hotel for four of us. Well, I headed straight to the cigar counter and asked a nice young lady if she would split it four ways. And I handed everybody their $2.50. We went in and had a big prime rib dinner, big dessert, paid our bill, and had money left over. The next morning, the coach comes straight to me and says, 'Where is my change?' I said, 'Coach, you always told us we should tip well when we represented the University of Maryland, we tipped well, and there's nothing left.'"

Who Needs Spikes When You've Got Moxy?

Frugal support extended to the team's equipment. During his senior season in the fall of 1940, Fields traveled alone to Michigan State, with no coach, to compete in the NCAA cross-country championships. The course was muddy and slippery, but all Fields had were flat-soled shoes. Everyone else, he says, was wearing spiked shoes.

After the competitors ran the first half-mile of the race on a softened cinder track, Fields was back in the pack. Once off the track, he slogged through the mud in his spikeless shoes and fell further behind.

But good fortune then struck for Fields. When they came out of the woods with about a mile to go, he noticed a concrete road next to the cinder path that was part of the course. With no spikes on his shoes, Field jumped on the road and made up a lot of space as his competitors struggled on the path.

"I started catching them in bunches," he said. Fields moved all the way up to second place. When they moved back onto the cinder track for the end of the race, Fields dropped to third. But it was a triumph nonetheless. With that result, Fields became Maryland's first cross-country All-American.

One week after leaving Maryland, Fields joined the Marine Corps. He later commanded troops at Iwo Jima, in the pivotal battle that helped the U.S win World War II. Fond memories of an accomplished athletic career helped Fields endure those tough times at war, and after a career in the Corps, Fields returned to Maryland some three decades later to create part two of an unmatched Terrapin legacy.

9

Coaching Instability

Frank Dobson, previously the head coach at Richmond for 20 years, had his best year as Maryland coach in 1937. Maryland finished the season at 8-2 and its only Southern Conference championship in the first half of the century.

It was a team of function more than flair. "Jarring" Jim Meade, a powerful running back and bruising linebacker, as well as punter, was the star for Maryland during that glorious year. Dobson gave much credit to two guards, Mike Surgent and Bill Wolfe, who opened holes for Meade all season.

Three Heads Are Not Better than One

Dobson was out as head coach following the 1939 season after winning just two games that year and the year before. Faber then returned as a part-time head coach for two seasons, winning only five games. In *Terrapin Tales: Maryland Football*, Faber called himself and his two assistants, Al Woods and Al Heagy, also part-time coaches, the "first three-headed coaching monster in the history of college football."

Compared to other Southern Conference schools, Maryland offered limited scholarship aid and did not recruit players as often. Woods appealed to Curley Byrd, then the school's president, that the football team needed more money to be competitive. Maryland's alumni and school paper urged Byrd to allocate more money to football.

Byrd relented in 1942 when he hired Clark Shaughnessy from Stanford for $10,500 per season. Considering Shaughnessy's reputation, Faber said he, Heagy and Woods willingly stepped down as head coaches. The three-headed monster retired with just five wins in two years. Heagy and Woods stayed on as assistants to Shaughnessy, while Faber and Heagy continued to coach lacrosse.

Shaughnessy, We Hardly Knew Ye

While head coach at Stanford, Shaughnessy turned a 1-7-1 team into an unbeaten Rose Bowl champion the following season.

Shaughnessy also changed Maryland's uniforms from black and gold to red and white. He preferred red because Stanford wore red and red was the color of his car. Critics to the change were quelled by that fact that Maryland's state seal is red, white, black and gold.

The Terps responded with a 7-2 season in Shaughnessy's first season. Led by quarterback Tommy Mont, their total offense was ranked 11th in the nation while passing was ranked fifth. The Terps won their first three games. Before the next game against VMI, Maryland's students gave the players a spirited send-off at the train station. But flooding rivers from heavy rains closed some bridges and delayed Maryland's departure. They arrived in Lexington, Virginia at 5:00 a.m. and suffered a 29-0 loss nine hours later.

Maryland rebounded with big wins over Western Maryland and a stunner over Florida in Griffith Stadium. In that game, Mont threw both touchdown passes, the second to Bob James, later the commissioner of the Atlantic Coast Conference.

Shaughnessy shocked and disappointed the Maryland faithful when he decided to back out of his five-year agreement and
coach the next season at Pittsburgh. The following two years under
head coach Clarence Spears yielded just five wins. Spears had
compiled an impressive winning record over a 25-year career at
six schools and had coached Bronko Nagurski, the Chicago Bears'
Hall of Fame running back.

His so-called "civilian-player program" during World War II
included 17-year-old freshmen, 4-Fs and a few veterans. Spears
was also the head of the physical education department with a
main responsibility of placing the school's male population in
top physical condition in case of a call-up to serve in the war. He
departed Maryland to work in private medicine.

In 1945, Byrd selected a former Alabama player and assistant coach named Paul "Bear" Bryant as Maryland's new football
coach.

The Bear Barely Left His Mark

Before taking the Maryland job, Bryant was head coach of
the Navy Preflight School team in Chapel Hill, North Carolina.
As the war was coming to an end, Bryant was told he would no
longer have a team. So he called a meeting of his players and told
them he would coach wherever they wanted to go to school next:
Georgia Tech or Alabama as an assistant coach, or Maryland as a
head coach. The players chose Maryland, and Bryant signed a
three-year deal for $9,000 a year.

Fifteen players from the Preflight School formed the nucleus
for Bryant's 1946 Maryland team. Bryant, who played one game
in college at Alabama with a broken leg, asked that his players be
as tough as he was when he played. He would often mix it up
with his players on the field to demonstrate a point.

Bryant called his early coaching days "my upchucking days"
for the times he would get sick before games along with his players. He also said he made some mistakes that year that cost the
team the national championship. "I was overanxious to prove

how good I was and I over-coached," said Bryant in *The Terrapins: Maryland Football*.

After Maryland won its first three games, there was talk of a New Year's Day bowl appearance. A loss the next week against Virginia Tech changed that chatter. Bryant took the blame for the loss, saying he took Tech lightly after they lost badly the previous week. Maryland finished the season 6-2-1, and with nine starters returning to the team, many held promise for the next season with Bryant leading the way.

But Bryant was the head coach at Kentucky the next season, and he blames Byrd for his abrupt departure. In *The Terrapins: Maryland Football*, Bryant said he discovered upon returning from a trip visiting family in Kentucky that Byrd had placed back on the team a player Bryant had suspended. Bryant also said Byrd was planning to fire one of his assistant coaches. While anguishing about the turn of events in his office, Bryant saw a telegram from the president of the University of Kentucky asking Bryant to contact him. He did and was offered the job at Kentucky.

Byrd said Bryant's departure caught him completely by surprise. Maryland football players and others reacted to the news by parading by torchlight to Byrd's house. Byrd, standing in his pajamas, said he wanted Bryant to stay but that Bryant had received a better offer and was leaving. Rather then attend classes the next morning, the students rallied in protest in front of the administration building.

Bryant appeared at the gathering to try and calm the masses. He said he was leaving willingly and that he was not taking any players with him. He also urged them to return to class.

Second Time No Charm for Shaughnessy

Clark Shaughnessy, who abruptly left College Park after a successful 1942 season, returned to Maryland as head coach in 1946, leaving behind three losing campaigns at Pittsburgh. His luck did not change in College Park.

He returned to Terpland showing a sign of remorse for how he had departed. "The rottenest thing I ever did in my life was to let Curley Byrd down the way I did in 1943, and I'm truly sorry," he told the media, according to the book *Kings of American Football*.

Byrd shared Shaughnessy's high salary with the Washington Redskins, who employed Shaughnessy as an advisor. Shaughnessy missed Maryland's three weeks of preseason to work with the Redskins. During the season, he helped the Redskins in the morning and coached Maryland in the afternoon, and some Redskins assistants helped coach at Maryland.

Shaughnessy's connection with the Redskins led to a unique arrangement between Maryland players and Redskins coaches. Backs Tommy Mont and Vic Turyn helped Shaughnessy call plays during Redskins games. Turyn claims he called three Redskins touchdowns in a game against Detroit.

The team was an uncomfortable mix of veteran players returning the war, such as Mont, and new recruits. Shaughnessy made the mix worse when he divided the team into two squads. Returning war players made up the big team, and Bryant's former players composed the little team.

Mont said players tried to resolve the differences with a team meeting. Due to injuries, Shaughnessy merged the two teams together for the game against Michigan State. Shaughnessy sent the team to East Lansing, Michigan, Thursday before the game without him. He stayed behind to work with the Redskins.

He next saw his players during a team meeting in a hotel the day of the game. According to the following report by Bob McLean in the *Washington Herald* newspaper, he probably did not like what he saw: "Maryland lost its football game in a Lansing hotel room today…It was a quiet Terp crew that greeted Shaughnessy…It was also a team that had been exploded in quarrels and a bit of inspiration from 'The Old Man' was what the Old Liners needed…and Shaughnessy tried to give it to them. But the Terps were deep in dissention and doubt."

After losing that game, Shaughnessy criticized the players, calling some bums and saying that some of the players who served in the military felt the world owed them something.

Those comments made Maryland officials uncomfortable. And it didn't help Shaughnessy that Byrd was unhappy with Maryland's two-team system and lack of discipline. Shaughnessy resigned in January, 1947. His replacement, Jim Tatum, would lead the Terps to one of the most glorious moments in their athletic history.

A Gift from Shaughnessy

In 1946, Shaughnessy formulated the idea to form the Maryland Educational Foundation as a football sponsors organization. It was set up as a scholarship fund for "deserving student athletes."

That led to the development that year of the Terrapin Club, the social segment of the MEC. Shaughnessy had implemented a similar program at the University of Tulane while coaching there.

Under Shaughnessy's plan, the group included a select number of former Maryland graduates who were deeply interested in the university. The plan set quota limits of 50 each from Baltimore and Washington and 25 each from Maryland's Western and Eastern Shores.

Each club member was charged a $25 fee to join. In 1950, club members voted to raise the membership limit to 250 from the original 150. They set an obligation to raise $20,000 per year for the Foundation. The following year, the Club reached its membership limit and its goal to raise the $20,000.

The goals of the Terrapin Club and its membership have increased dramatically since then. In fiscal year 2002, membership in the Terrapin Club topped 7,000 and the Foundation raised $8.5 million, $2 million more than its goal for that year. Interest in obtaining tickets for men's basketball games at the team's new arena, Comcast Center, fueled the higher-than-expected donations that year. Supporters receive tickets to the games if they donate a certain amount to the Foundation. The Terrapin Club's goal for 2003 was again 6.5 million.

Kehoe the Conquerer

Jim Kehoe was already a winner before he took over as Maryland's head track and field coach in 1947. As a distance runner from 1936 to 1940, Kehoe set school records in the two-mile and the half-mile and was undefeated in dual meet competition. He also won Southern Conference titles in the indoor and outdoor 880-yard run in 1940. His outdoor school record time of 1:50.7 lasted for 23 years.

Kehoe developed a championship track team within five years of becoming head coach. He won Maryland's first outdoor conference title in 1951 and its first indoor conference title a year later. That began a string of 48 Southern Conference and ACC Conference titles through 1969. His conference record is unmatched in the school's athletic history.

Jim Kehoe

Only once, in 1955, did Maryland not win a conference indoor or outdoor track title under Kehoe. The Terps lost both meets to North Carolina, by 1.25 points outdoors and one point indoors.

"Dammit, I'll never get over that," the still-competitive Kehoe said in the spring of 2003, at the age of 85 and nearly a half-century after the losses.

Kehoe used that competitive fire to not only get the most out of his athletes as a coach, but to later rebuild the school's athletic program as athletic director.

Big Man Tatum

Jim Tatum is the most successful coach in Maryland football history, and not only because he guided the Terps to their only national championship. In nine seasons as head coach, Tatum compiled a .815 winning percentage (73-15-4) second only to Ralph Friedgen's .833 through his first two seasons in 2001 and 2002. Under Tatum, Maryland also won the Southern Conference championship in 1951, during Tatum's only undefeated season.

Tatum had been head coach at Oklahoma for one season before he took the Maryland job. Oklahoma released Tatum from his three-year contract only after assistant Bud Wilkinson agreed to take over for Tatum.

When Byrd went looking for a new coach after Shaugnesssy resigned, he met with both Tatum and Wilkinson. He told them either one could have the job and left it up to them to decide who would take it. They decided Tatum was the one.

Byrd first offered a head coaching job to Tatum in 1942. Byrd says he and Oklahoma offered head coaching jobs to Tatum for the 1946 season. But after Harvard coach Dick Harlow agreed to take the Maryland job, Byrd offered Tatum a job as an assistant coach.

Tatum opted for Oklahoma and led the Sooners to a 7-3 record and a win over North Carolina State in the Gator Bowl, but there was some talk that Oklahoma's alumni didn't think Tatum won often enough. Meantime, Harlow ultimately decided not to take the Maryland job, leading to Shaughnessy's disastrous one-year return campaign.

Byrd gave the 33-year-old Tatum a $12,000-per-year contract for five years. He also gave Tatum complete control of the football team and made him athletic director as well. The era of part-time coaches was over. Stability had arrived and would reign over Maryland football for nine years.

The Charmer, the Recruiter, and the Organizer

Tatum, who was a tackle at North Carolina in the early 1930s, was known as "Big Jim" for his size, 6'4" and 240 pounds. He was also called "Sunny Jim" for his gregarious nature, which helped him recruit players.

While recruiting Ed Modzelewski in a Pennsylvania steel-milling town, Tatum attended a Catholic church service with Modzelewski's family although he was not Catholic. Modzelewski remembered how Tatum placed $20 in the collection plate when a 50-cent donation was worthy of high praise.

Tatum's tendency toward random talk and opinions at times got him into trouble. Wrote one author about Tatum: "He has been variously described as ruthless and soft-hearted, shrewd and tactless, candid and hypocritical. Actually, all of these adjectives apply."

If he liked someone, he treated him very well. Tatum gave some of his clothes to his center and All-American Bob Pellegrini because he didn't have any money. Tatum allowed another player to sleep in the basement of his house.

On the field, Tatum was known as an intense, meticulous planner who stressed defense. He limited practices to one hour, 45 minutes, a change compared to practices under Shaughnessy, some of which lasted until 10 at night. He and his coaches were known for working 16-hour days. When he took the job, he said he wanted to schedule teams from the Big Ten, the Big Six, the Ivy League and the Southeastern Conference.

Tatum's goal was to have a team that would make Maryland proud by 1950. He surpassed his expectations from the beginning.

Running back Lu Gambino scored eight touchdowns in Maryland's first three games in 1947, all victories. Gambino sat the bench under Shaughnessy, but Tatum took Gambino on as a project, and it worked. Gambino finished fourth in the nation in scoring with 96 points and 16 touchdowns and was a first-team all Southern Conference selection. He helped Maryland finish the season 7-2-2, including a tie with Georgia in the Gator Bowl.

But Gambino's success at Maryland was short-lived. In 1948, the Southern Conference declared Gambino ineligible, saying he had played too many years of college football.

Gambino said later in *The Terrapins: Maryland Football* that it was a "crooked" decision. He said the rules allowed four years of eligibility when players returned from the war. He had played two years at Indiana before the war and two years for Maryland after the war.

Gambino picked Maryland in part to be closer to his mother, who was living in Baltimore after his father died. Gambino said Indiana was "50 times" better than Maryland, which he called a "cow school." Still, he had vowed to help Maryland "beat the rest of them so bad, it hurt." Maryland lost its last three games in 1948 and ended the season 6-4.

The 1949 season was a different story. The Terps' only loss was to Michigan State in front of 35,000 at East Lansing. For the first time, the Terps received a national ranking.

National Notice

Stan Lavine, who would later serve as the football team's orthopedist, saw most of his action as quarterback in 1949, helping

Maryland win its last seven games. Against 15th-ranked Boston University, he came off the bench at the end of the game to direct the offense to the winning score. Entering the ninth game against Miami, Lavine led the team in total offense and scoring. To that point, they had scored more points than any other Maryland team.

The Associated Press placed Maryland 14th by the end of the season, after the Terps beat Missouri in the Gator Bowl to finish 9-1. Guard Bob Ward, voted the game's most valuable player, said in the book *The Terrapins: Maryland Football* that winning the game "was just like going to heaven…I remember the facilities were terrible, the water leaked from the showers into the locker room. But it was our first bowl game. You never forget it."

Ward Wows 'Em

Jim Tatum called Ward the greatest football player he had seen and the best he had coached. Ward weighed only 178 pounds, but he solidified both Maryland's offensive and defensive lines with a rare level of intensity and aggressiveness. His speed and quickness offset his relative lack of size.

"I saw days where they would try to triple-team him," said teammate Dick Modzelewski, a tackle, in the book *The Terrapins: Maryland Football*. "They could not do it…it was freeing everyone else to make tackles."

After serving in World War II, Ward was planning to play football at Alabama. But Tatum stepped in and recruited Ward to attend Maryland, and Ward, preferring to play for a more northern school, said yes.

After meeting Ward, Tatum was reluctant to use a scholarship on a lineman of his relative small size. "He looked at me and I could tell he was disappointed," said Ward in the book *The Terrapins: Maryland Football*. "The first thing he said was, 'I thought you were bigger than that.'" So Tatum convinced Ward to enter Maryland on the GI Bill, which paid for his education.

Ward achieved several firsts by the time he finished his football career at Maryland. He was a first-team All-American on defense in 1950. As a senior the next season, Tatum asked Ward to play just offense to help guide an inexperienced line, and he was a first-team All-American that year as well. He was also the first Maryland player to be picked Southern Conference Player of the Year.

But Ward said that another award was the most important of all those he received as a Maryland football player: His teammates voted him the team's most valuable player for four consecutive years.

Aided by back Bob Shemonski scoring 97 points in 1950, then a school record, and averaging nine yards every time he touched the ball, Maryland finished the 1950 season with a respectable 7-2-1 record.

Hot Dogs

Before the 1951 season, Jim Tatum, with typical bravado, said that year's team had the talent to be the best team he ever coached. Maryland lived up to its coach's hype, finishing the year 10-0 co-champion of the Southern Conference and, in many people's minds, the national champion.

Maryland was involved in only one really close game that season, a 14-7 win over Coach Tatum's alma mater, North Carolina, in their fourth game. It was the first time Tatum beat his former school and the first time for the Terps since 1926.

Some of Maryland's wins that year were so dominant, that their starters often sat the entire second half of games. One game, the players were served hot dogs on the bench.

Ward was the headline player for Maryland that year, as an offensive guard. The defense yielded only 62 points that year. With Dick Modzeleswki anchoring the dominant defensive line, brother Ed helped the offense score 353 points, setting a school record.

Junior quarterback Jack Scarbath threw the winning touchdown to Lou Weidensaul in the Carolina game.

Scarbath is an integral part of Maryland football history. In his first start, he scored the first touchdown in the new Byrd Stadium on a 21-yard run in the first game of the 1950 season. In two seasons, Scarbath led the Terps to a 24-4-1 record. In 1952, he was a consensus first-team All-American and was runner-up in the Heisman Trophy balloting.

To prepare his team for the next game against LSU, Tatum used a wet ball in practice to simulate the effects of Louisiana's notorious humidity. He also encouraged his boys to blow off some steam in New Orleans, taking the players to the lively city before the game. According to Ed Modzelewski, the curfew Tatum set for the players was largely ignored, so Tatum sent out a recovery crew in cabs to collect tardy members of the team. Tatum told them to forget about the incident and to approach the game as the second part of the season. Maryland won the game 27-0.

Deny the Bowl Bid, or Bye-Bye

After comfortably winning its next two games, Maryland received a bid to the Sugar Bowl. Under normal circumstances, accepting the bid would be an easy decision. But in September, the presidents of the Southern Conference voted to recommend that a ban be placed on bowl games. The presidents felt the pressure to win a bowl game could lead to recruiting abuses.

Clemson asked the presidents for permission to accept an invitation to play in the Orange Bowl that season. The presidents met in Richmond, Virginia on December 15 to discuss the matter.

At the meeting, Byrd strongly opposed the recommendation. He said no team had been refused permission to play in a bowl game before. He also felt Maryland was not legally restricted to follow the recommendation, since it was not formally adopted by the conference. Further, he said instituting the recommendation at that time would amount to changing a rule in the middle of the season. Byrd also reasoned that the conference had previously allowed its schools to go to postseason games.

Fourteen schools voted for the resolution, which was introduced by the University of North Carolina. Maryland, Clemson and South Carolina voted against it. The vote prompted a scathing column by Jack Horner of the *Durham Morning Herald*. In the story, Horner wrote: "How have bowl games become such evils overnight? I haven't heard of any bowl games being thrown, or the points being shaved. No other conference bans participation in postseason games...I think Duke and North Carolina ought to be ashamed of themselves for being ringleaders in the 'bowl ban' movement. They ought to go stand in the corner."

Maryland and Clemson ignored the resolution. The next year, Southern Conference teams were forbidden to play the two schools. Maryland and Clemson were teams without a conference for one season.

A Sweet Sugar Bowl Debut

Maryland's preparation for the 1952 Sugar Bowl against Tennessee had not gone smoothly. Bad weather before Christmas created poor practice conditions. Their plane arrived five hours late to Biloxi, Mississippi, where they were scheduled to practice for a week. Left end Paul Lindsay broke a hand, and running back Ralph Felton injured ligaments in his right knee.

Before the game, Tatum told his players, "We're like the little boy who said: 'Hell no, I'm not the toughest kid in the neighborhood, but I can lick the kid who is.'"

In front of 85,000 fans, Maryland led 21-0 after 20 minutes and held on to win 28-13. Ed Fullerton, playing in place of the injured Felton, was involved in Maryland's first two scores. He ran three yards after a quick count from Scarbath for Maryland's first score and threw a pass to halfback Bob Shemonski for the Terps' next score. This despite having a less-than-glowing reputation as a passer.

"He could throw a ball into a shower and not get it wet,' said Scarbath in the book *The Terrapins: Maryland Football*. Tennessee had lined up with a four-man secondary. Against that defensive formation, Maryland's game plan called for a halfback pass. Once, Scarbath changed the play at the line of scrimmage, and Fullerton told him he was not going to throw the pass.

"I said, 'Yes, you are,'" said Scarbath in that book. "It was a terrible pass, but Shemonski caught it. For years, Fullerton has claimed he taught me to pass."

Fullerton also intercepted two passes and recovered a fumble in the game, but Modzelewski won Player of the Game honors after gaining 153 yards on 28 carries, an effort that prompted Neyland to call him the best fullback he had ever seen.

Despite winning the game, Maryland could not claim the top national ranking, since the polls had closed before the Sugar Bowl was played. They finished the season with a number three national ranking.

Keep It in the Family

Modzelewski's effort in the Sugar Bowl proved to be a proper payout to Tatum for the effort he and his staff put into recruiting and landing the West Natrona, Pennsylvania native. Modzelewski did not like the school after his visit to College Park, and he was more interested in attending Penn State or Michigan State.

After preseason practice had started, Modzelewski decided to attend Michigan State. When he called Tatum on a Sunday to tell him about his decision, Tatum told Modzelewski not to do anything. When Modzelewski got back from church, he received a call from George Barkley, Tatum's assistant. Calling from an airport in Pittsburgh, Barkley asked Modzelewski to wait at his house.

Barkley hailed from West Natrona, and his sister taught at Modzelewski's high school. Their families were close friends. At times, Barkley stayed at Modzelewski's house during visits to West Natrona.

Modzelewski changed his mind and decided to attend Penn State. But when Barkley babysat at Modzelewski's house one evening during the visit, he changed his mind again and finally decided on Maryland.

"I went back to school with him," said Modzelewski in *The Terrapins: Maryland Football*. "I stayed in a dorm in old Byrd Stadium and I woke up the first night and saw [cock]roaches. I said 'That was it,' but Tatum took me to his house for three days and I finally decided to stay."

Ed Modzelewski remembers a similarly compelling tale of how Tatum convinced his younger brother, Dick, to attend Maryland. Dick Modzelewski liked Maryland when he visited the school, but he was homesick during his visit. He decided to go to Notre Dame.

Tatum panicked when he heard Dick was not going to attend Maryland, so he called the state police to find Ed, who had stayed near the school that summer to work in rural Virginia.

Ed often slept in a truck at night. "They flashed a light in my face and told me Tatum wanted me at Maryland right away," said Ed in *The Terrapins: Maryland Football*. "They drove me to his office, where he had Dick. He told Dick that only priests and lawyers go to Notre Dame and that he wasn't smart enough to be a lawyer and he sure knew he wasn't going to be a priest. He brought our whole family down for a week so Dick wouldn't be lonely. It was the first time my dad ever saw a television. Dick must have threatened to leave 10 times that year."

But Dick stayed, building possibly the most significant sibling legacy in the history of Terp athletics. Ed's career rushing yards record (1913) lasted 23 years and he was a second-team All-American in 1951. Dick was a two-time All-American and the Outland Trophy winner in 1952 as the best lineman in college football.

See Ya, Ship

The men's basketball team suffered a string of losing seasons from 1940-41 to 1945-46. Football coach Bear Bryant then helped provide some temporary relief to the program for the 1946-47 season. Some of the football players he brought to Maryland from the North Carolina Preflight team also played basketball. They helped Maryland to a 14-10 record, 9-4 in the Southern Conference. But Maryland lost in the first round of the conference tournament to NC State. It was a disappointing end to Burton Shipley's last season as men's basketball coach.

But the abrupt end did not diminish Shipley's legacy as an entertaining, eccentric and effective basketball coach.

During one game at Navy, he brought 30 candy bars to feed his players at halftime, but instead ate them all himself during the game. During a trip south to play Duke, NC State and Virginia, Maryland spent the night in a gymnasium building after playing the Wolfpack. Overnight, melting snow dripped through the roof, prompting Shipley to take his team back to Maryland without stopping in Charlottesville to play Virginia. Athletic director Curley Byrd reprimanded Shipley for the move.

Shipley stories extended to the baseball field. The coach more than once moved a snow fence that served at the outfield boundaries to fit the talents of his outfielders.

"If he had someone who could run and catch fly balls, he'd open up that area," said Elton "Jack" Jackson, Shipley's assistant and later Maryland's head baseball coach. "And depending on what kind of hitters he had, he'd move it in or out."

Before a game with Virginia, Shipley told his team to run for the team bus if he blew a whistle during the game. After an umpire called a Virginia player safe on a play at second base, Shipley asked his infielder if he had tagged the man in time. After the player said yes, Shipley blew the whistle, the players ran to the bus and Maryland was gone minutes later, leaving a stunned Virginia team still on the field.

A player Shipley cut from the baseball team told Shipley he would be sorry for what he did. Later, during a practice, a man with a rifle appeared on the top of Ritchie Coliseum, near the practice field. He fired shots at the first baseman and the short-stop, who both fell to the ground.

The man then told Shipley the next one was for him. "I told you I'd get you for cutting me," said the man, as recorded in the book *Maryland Basketball*. Moments after Shipley dove into the dugout, the struck players stood up, laughing. They were hit by blanks. Shipley was the victim of a prank.

After Shipley's departure, the basketball team endured three losing seasons under Coach Flucie Stewart. Next came Bud Millikan, whose 17-year reign as coach created consistent confer-ence respectability and the first flickering of national attention for the program.

Champs of the Country
and a New Conference

After leaving the Southern Conference in 1953, Maryland helped form the Atlantic Coast Conference, which began play the next year along with South Carolina, North Carolina, Clemson, North Carolina State, Duke and Wake Forest.

Maryland lost some good players for the 1953 season, including Scarbath and Dick Modzelewski, but the Terps were ranked as high as number one in some preseason polls. Maryland ended the regular season undefeated for the second time in three years.

Its only blemish was 7-0 loss to Oklahoma in the Orange Bowl. Shutout wins over Mississippi and Alabama, both ranked number 11 when they played the Terps, to close out the season highlighted the most successful campaign of any Maryland football team.

Bernie Faloney, a two-year defensive starter and a backup to Scarbath, took over as starting quarterback. Faloney played four sports in high school and liked football the best. He received only one offer to play football in college; some thought he was too small to play college football. But he eagerly accepted the Maryland offer and became one of its more versatile players in the program's history.

Maryland was co-champion of the Atlantic Coast Conference in the first year of the conference.

Faloney was forced out of the Alabama game early due to a knee injury, but the Terps shut out the Crimson Tide, securing a number one ranking at the end of the regular season and the school's first national championship. A jubilant Tatum told his team the news as they ate their traditional end-of- the-season spaghetti dinner. The team later enjoyed a parade and luncheon in downtown Washington in their honor.

Faloney rested his injured knee for three weeks during preparation for the Orange Bowl. He had resumed practice with the team in Miami Beach, the site of the game. But on December 29, he hurt the knee again on the last play of practice while running the option, despite the fact that Tatum played defensive end on the play to help protect Faloney.

With Faloney out of the game, Charley Boxold was named the Terps' starting quarterback in the Sugar Bowl. Boxold enrolled at Maryland as a running back. He broke his leg in the only previous game he played in 1952. But he had some success as a quarterback. He threw his first pass as a Terp in 1953 for a touchdown in the season opener against Missouri.

With Faloney out of the game, Maryland was still favored over the fourth-ranked Sooners. But the Terps could not adjust to the loss of Faloney and a new game plan. Twice they failed to score with first down within Oklahoma's 10-yard line. Faloney even got in for five plays late in the third quarter with the Terps behind, but to no avail. They lost, 7-0.

"I felt useless, helpless," said Faloney in *The Terrapins: Maryland Football*. "I could have just as well sat at the hot dog stand."

Despite the bowl loss, the Terps held on to their number one ranking, since final rankings were determined before the bowl games were played. It was the only number one ranking at the end of the season in the history of the program.

The Terps received additional national honors that season. Faloney was a second-team All-American, and teammate Stan Jones, a tackle, was a unanimous first-team All-American.

Bye, Bye, Byrd

The Sugar Bowl loss was an unfitting sendoff for Byrd, who before the game had resigned as school president to run for governor of Maryland. Byrd sat on the bench during the Sugar Bowl.

Maryland had 260 students when Byrd enrolled in the school in 1905. When he took over as president, the school boasted 3,400 students. When he retired, Maryland had 15,700 students. Byrd never became Maryland governor, but his legacy at the University of Maryland is unmatched.

Millikan Molds Terps

When Jim Tatum, Maryland's athletic director and football coach, hired Bud Millikan as head basketball coach in 1950, Millikan was a 29-year-old high school coach in Iowa. But he was much more accomplished than that title implied. Millikan had worked as the freshman coach and assistant varsity coach for Henry Iba at Oklahoma A&M and won a national title with the team in 1946. He also was a guard on the Merryville High School team in Missouri, which won 53 consecutive games and one state title.

Millikan, aided by the recruiting of Jim Tatum, mastered winning records during his first three seasons. Basketball players chose Maryland in part due to Tatum's work bringing football players to the school. Tom Young, a guard for the Terps who later coached Rutgers to the NCAA Final Four in 1976, said he attended Maryland in part because eight football players from his high school went there.

The Shue Fits

Tatum had nothing to do with Millikan signing Gene Shue, the coach's most prized recruit during his early years. A supporter of Maryland athletics informed Millikan about Shue's talents.

"In those days, you could try recruits out, have them play against other players," said Millikan. "I told him right there I wanted him. He had a lot of basketball sense and was a hard worker. He had talent."

Several schools, mostly from the Baltimore-Washington area, recruited Shue out of Baltimore's Towson Catholic High School. Shue wanted to attend Georgetown, but he struggled at a tryout there and was placed on a waiting list.

"When I went there for the tryout, I didn't play well at all," said Shue. His tryout for Maryland was much better.

"Georgetown was the biggest competition to get him," said Millikan. "Georgetown was recruiting heavily out of the northeast, they had a guy or two who was indecisive, and they kept putting Gene off, waiting for a decision from the other players. I said to him, 'I told you from the word go that I want you at Maryland. I don't think Georgetown is being fair to you and I don't think you're being fair to Maryland.'"

Millikan gave Shue 10 days to give him an answer. He never regretted his decision.

"When Bud came in, he turned the whole program around," said Shue. "Up to that point, Maryland was a football school. Basketball until Bud got there was doing nothing. He did a remarkable job. In his first year, it was one of the greatest coaching jobs I've ever seen. He took a ragtag bunch of players and did great with them."

Shue accepted a deal at Maryland that required him to work odd jobs in his dormitory at Ritchie Coliseum, where the Terps played their home games, and later sweep the floor of the coliseum in exchange for a scholarship. He earned a full scholarship his senior year.

"We used to come down and turn the lights on and play basketball late at night," said Shue. "Basketball was our life in those days. And with Bud, just about every free minute we were playing basketball."

Shue was considered a complete player, He defended the other team's best player, was a sturdy rebounder and adept at the two-handed set shot. Shue, who left Maryland in 1954, was the leading scorer in Maryland history until Tom McMillen broke the record in 1974. He was also Maryland's first All-American since Bosey Berger in 1932.

During his junior season in 1952-53, Shue scored 40 points in the Southern Conference semifinal loss to Wake Forest and was the tournament MVP.

The next season was full of milestone moments. Their 23 wins marked the first time a Terp basketball team earned more than 20 wins. For the first time in history, they broke into the national ranking, soaring as high as 13th before finishing the season at 20. Shue played a big part in the Terps' success that season. His 654 points broke his own record. He made first-team All-ACC and was a first-team All-American.

The Terps finished second their first year in the ACC conference with a 7-2 record. Their had high hopes of winning the first conference tournament. But it was not to be. Despite Shue's 25 points, Maryland lost in the tournament semifinal to Wake Forest. Duke, the tournament favorite, also lost in the semifinals. Charles "Lefty" Driesell, Maryland's basketball coach nearly two decades later, was a member of that Duke team.

Shue, a two-time All-American, departed Maryland as the school's first high-profile player during the dawn of a new era in Maryland basketball. And his success continued when he left Maryland. Shue played 10 years in the NBA with the Philadelphia Warriors and was an NBA All-Star five times. He was also twice named NBA Coach of the Year.

Not Slow, But Deliberate

Millikan preferred a deliberate pace during an era of basketball dominated by up-and-down-the-court action. Just before the ACC tournament in 1953, several teams reportedly threatened to not play the Terps to protest their slow style.

"I don't remember anyone turning us down because of the way we played," said Millikan. "If they didn't want to play us, they figured we'd be tough to beat. What does style have to do with it?"

In the book *Maryland Basketball*, Wake Forest coach Murray Greason said, "You practice running every day, so why play a team that wants to walk?"

"That's a bad rap in some ways," said Millikan. "We would gain possession of the ball, and we wanted to get it to the other end the floor as quickly as we could. But we wanted to be sure we had possession of the ball as soon as we get there. We didn't want to lose the ball. We wanted to take the ball to the baseline and if we didn't' have a good shot, then take it out front. We probably worked a bit longer to wait for the good shot, but if we had a good shot, we put it up."

Close to a Repeat

It was tough for Tatum to match the national championship of the 1953 season, but he came close during his last two years as Maryland's coach. The Terps received a number three preseason ranking in 1954, but ended up eighth in the final poll after two losses and a tie against Wake Forest in their first five games. They ended the season on a high note, beating Missouri 74-13.

The beginning of the season was again critical for the Terps in 1955. A 7-0 win over number one-ranked UCLA helped catapult Maryland to 10-0 regular season and a number two ranking at the end of the season. A 20-6 loss to number one Oklahoma in the Orange Bowl placed the Terps third in the final Associated Press poll.

A key player for the Terps that year was lineman Bob Pellegrini. Pellegrini came to Maryland as a quarterback. As a sophomore and junior, the 6'2", 215-pound Pellegrini played offensive guard and linebacker and was one of the best in the country. He later played that position with the world champion Philadelphia Eagles. Tatum switched Pellegrini to center his senior year, a position he had never played before. That year, Pellegrini was named the ACC Player of the Year.

Pellegrini was a consensus All-American, Lineman of the Year and a National Football Foundation Hall of Fame inductee in 1996.

A Boon for Basketball

As senior captain of the 1955-56 basketball team, John Sandbower had the honor of being the first Maryland player to run on the court that year at the new Student Activities Building, later known as Cole Field House.

"I was the first player out of that runway," said Sandbower in the book *Maryland Basketball*. "It was one of the most exciting feelings I've ever had in my life."

When the building opened, it was considered the second largest building of its type in the East. Only Madison Square Garden in New York City was bigger. Bob Kessler scored the first two points in the building in the 12-point opening win over Virginia.

The opening of the new arena signaled the end of the boxing-basketball doubleheaders in Ritchie Coliseum that were once a prime athletic ticket at Maryland. By that time, the appeal of intercollegiate boxing had faded, due in part to the mounting number of deaths in the ring.

Maryland mastered winning records during its first two years in Cole Field House.

*The Student Activity Building in 1955,
later known as Cole Field House.*

The Terps lost only two games in the newly named Cole Field House that season. One was to North Carolina, who were riding a 16-game win streak on the way to an undefeated season and a national championship. The allure of the Frank McGuire-coached Tar Heels prompted the first sellout in Cole Field House history. The Tar Heels won in double overtime by four points.

Two newcomers to the team provided a boost the following year to give Millikan the most noted team in his career. Al Bunge, a sturdy six-feet-eight former football player, gave Maryland a strong, if not flashy, presence under the basket at a time when big men started playing more important roles in a team's success. And Charlie McNeil was considered one of the top sophomores in the country. Further, playmaking guard Tom Young returned after some time in the army to co-captain the team.

Maryland showed early it was primed for a prolific season. The Terps topped number one-ranked Kentucky, 71-62, in the third game of the season before 10,800 at Cole Field House. More than 15,000 fans watched Maryland beat number three-ranked

North Carolina in Cole later that year. Maryland lost just once at home, to North Carolina State.

The Terps finished with a 9-4 conference record in the regular season, which looked better considering the ACC included four teams among the nation's top 17. Maryland received a number four seed in the conference tournament in Raleigh and won by four points in the opening round game against Virginia. In the semifinal, Maryland had a 15-point lead against Duke in the second half before Duke stormed back. A left-handed hook shot by McNeil forced the game into overtime, and Maryland won by five points.

The Terps faced North Carolina in the final, and it was another classic game. Maryland was down by 13 late in the half, but they won the game by making 40 of 52 free throws in the game—including 25 in the last four minutes—and shooting 61 percent from the field.

Thirteen hundred students traveled north to Madison Square Garden in New York City to watch Maryland play its first NCAA tournament game against Boston College. Young led the Terps with 25 points as they won the game, 86-63.

In the East Region semifinal against fifth-ranked Temple, Bunge, who battled an intestinal disorder throughout his Maryland career, blamed the illness for his bad play. And Young said he couldn't make a shot. The Terps lost, 71-67, despite making 23 of 28 free throws. They beat Manhattan 59-55 in a region consolation game and for the first time finished the season with more than 2,000 points. Their number six national ranking at season's end would not be surpassed for 15 years.

Millikan called that team the most rewarding squad he coached at Maryland. "It was a hell of a good ball club," said Millikan. "They did what they needed to do to win. We had great leadership—Tom Young, and John Nacincik. They played well together. People could come off the bench to do it for us."

Royal Treatment

The Terps' football team struggled after Jim Tatum left. Former star Terp quarterback Tommy Mont coached the team from 1956 to 1958 to two losing seasons and one .500 season. It didn't help Mont that Maryland president Wilson Elkins took away 14 percent of the football scholarships as part of his effort to place more emphasis on academics.

Nugent, though, did enjoy one experience no other Maryland coach can claim. On October 19, 1957, he coached Maryland in a game attended by Queen Elizabeth II and Prince Phillip of England.

Shortly after she gained the throne, the queen mentioned interest in attending a college football game while she visited the United States. Elkins invited her to attend a Maryland game against North Carolina in College Park.

The queen and the prince made a grand entrance. Their motorcade proceeded into the stadium through its tunnel, drove on part of the track around the end zone nearest the scoreboard and stopped behind the Maryland bench just in front of their seats. They watched the game in a covered box set up in the bottom rows opposite the 50-yard line.

Maryland officials could not erect seats behind the scoreboard-side end zone because protocol disallowed spectators from sitting with their backs to the queen as she entered.

They also made seating adjustments to accommodate the close to 400 media that attended the game. A second floor was added to the press box atop the stadium. Society editors from the Commonwealth countries sat in a row of seats on the track, the only time that was done for a Maryland football game.

"They were tickled to death," said Jack Zane, Maryland's longtime sports information director, who was an assistant in that office during the game. "Most of them had never been to a college football game. That was prime seating for them." The 21-14 Maryland victory in front of 43,000 spectators offered more significance for Terps fans beyond showcasing the team's talent to British Royalty. The coach of North Carolina was Jim Tatum. It was Tatum's first game in College Park since leaving the Terps in 1955.

After the game, Maryland players placed Nugent on their shoulders and carried him over to the queen's box, where he chatted with the queen and prince. The big day for the queen continued after the football game ended. While driving home, down the aptly named Queens Chapel Road a couple miles south of the campus, she asked to stop at a local grocery store.

"She said she always wanted to go into a U.S. grocery store," said Zane.

The Nuances of Nugent

The crafty and unpredictable coach Tom Nugent led the Terps for the next seven seasons, including winning campaigns in 1961 and 1962. Nugent was nicknamed the Magician for reviving programs at Florida State and the Virginia Military Academy. And his bag of tricks was full.

Once he loaded his team on buses and told them they were headed to a secret workout. They went to a swimming party instead. A few days later, he put the team through a 90-minute workout on what was supposed to be an easy day.

Players provided drama as well during Nugent's time as head coach. Darryl Hill, Maryland's first black football player, broke the ACC record for touchdowns in 1963. Field goal kicker Bernardo Bramson, a three-year varsity player until 1966, changed his uniform number during games to correspond with his kicking points.

In a 1964 win over Navy, lineman Jerry Fishman made an obscene gesture toward the Midshipmen in the stands when he left the game, prompting the end of football relations between the schools.

After improving to 7-2 in 1961 following a win over Wake Forest, the Terps received an invitation to play in the Gator Bowl. Nugent said Maryland would accept the bid only if it beat Virginia in its final regular-season game. Maryland lost 28-16 and did not play in a bowl game that season. Maryland did not come close to receiving a bowl bid for another 11 seasons.

One That Got Away

Mike Sandusky was a second-team All-American tackle at Maryland in 1955 and a football Academic All-American in 1956. He was also an All-American heavyweight wrestler for the Terps in 1957.

John McHugh, a teammate of Sandusky, and later head wrestling coach, remembers how Sandusky was the victim of a questionable decision by a referee that year at the NCAA tournament. The decision, McHugh says, prevented Sandusky from advancing to the final match.

Sandusky and his competitor from Oklahoma had wrestled to a 1-1 tie. As McHugh explains, in the case of a tie, the wrestler who has earned more riding time, or has stayed atop the other wrestler longer, usually receives the win.

Sandusky tied the match early in the third of three periods. McHugh says Sandusky had earned at least a minute and a half of riding time advantage over his competitor. So Sandusky wrestled conservatively the rest of the match, thinking he would get the victory as a result of his riding time advantage.

"After the match, we told Mike he got the win," said McHugh.

The referee, aided by a technical malfunction, did not see it that way. McHugh says that year was the first time the NCAA had used an electric timer to keep track of the riding time. After the match the referee walked over to the table to consult with the riding time official, who could not provide an accurate result. Someone had kicked the wire loose on the timer. McHugh said the official emphatically told the referee Sandusky had the advantage in riding time.

"It's the referee's decision after a tie, and he decided to give the other wrestler the win," said McHugh.

"Apparently he made a decision on who was more aggressive in the last minute. As soon as the referee raised the other wrestler's arm, [coach] Sully Krause went after him. He chased him out of the gym. Sully was hard on referees at the nationals."

McHugh, however, won some revenge the next season. He wrestled the referee's son in an NCAA preliminary round match.

"I was beating the guy, and there was a timeout during the match," said McHugh. "Sully said, 'If you don't beat this guy, you're gonna have to wrestle me on the sidelines.' I went out and increased the lead after that and beat him."

A Firm Hold on the Conference

In the 63 years Maryland has sported a wrestling team, one man stands out as the program's Papa Bear.

During William E. "Sully" Krouse's career as wrestling coach from 1947 until 1978, Maryland won 20 ACC titles and two Southern Conference crowns. He coached 155 ACC individual champions, six All-Americans and two NCAA champions.

Krouse, who died from cancer at age 83 in 2000, helped start wrestling at Maryland as a student in 1940 and was runner-up for the Southern Conference heavyweight title that year, when

Maryland finished 6-1 under head coach Jim Douglas. It took six years for Krouse to win Maryland's first Southern Conference team title, in 1952. They also won the title in 1953. After that, the Terps dominated conference competition. Maryland wrestlers won the next 17 consecutive conference titles and were unbeaten in ACC competition from 1954 to 1969. A second-place ACC finish in 1970 broke that streak. The Terps won the next four conference crowns, but have not won one since. During their time of dominance, Maryland won every weight class in the conference tournament at least three times. Krouse also served as tournament director for three NCAA wrestling championships. His first event in 1972, at Cole Field House, set a record for attendance at 42,500. Krouse's larger-than-life personality overshadowed his girth.

"Sully was a great guy," said Bob Kopinksy, a national champion in 1965. "You learned a lot from Sully about life, just from watching him and being around him. He would always have something to say about getting along with people. Sully would be the first to admit he didn't know a lot about wrestling, but he knew people and he'd support you and back you. Sully treated me as fair as anyone in my life."

John McHugh was a two-time ACC champion for Krouse in the mid-1950s and later was an assistant for Krouse, before he took over the program in the late 1970s.

"Sully came in late one day for practice," said McHugh. "He forgot to put a belt on. He was standing there in the wrestling room and a wrestler bumped into him, and his pants fell down. He had these skinny little legs and no body. We all got a good laugh out of that. He said to me, 'How do you like the way I broke the tension in the room today?' He always had a lot of jokes for practice."

Saunas and Sully

One year Maryland traveled to Navy for a wrestling match. Krouse asked the Navy coach, Ed Perry, if his athletes could use the school's sauna to help them make weight. According to Bob Kopinksy, a national champion in 1965 under Krause, Perry said the sauna did not work.

"I think he was being honest, but Sully didn't believe him," said Kopinsky.

When Navy later went to Maryland for another match, Krouse had a plan of retribution for Perry. "Sully said, 'Perry wants to use my sauna, I'll show him,'" said Kopinksy.

Krouse turned the sauna off and placed a large block of ice in the middle of the room.

"He's waiting for Perry to ask him to use the sauna," said Kopinksy. "It turned out none of the wrestlers needed to lose weight, and Perry never asked him. Sully almost died that Ed Perry didn't see the block of ice in the sauna. Part of it was a joke, but he was really pissed off."

An Office as Big as the Man Himself

When Krouse was coach, Maryland's wrestlers trained in a room on the second floor of Cole Field House, behind the basket where the players walk onto the court. Krouse's office was one floor down, and as Kopinsky remembers, it was almost as big as the wrestling room.

"It would make the office of the president of the university look like a janitor's office," said Kopinksy. "It had knotty pine wood paneling, wood furniture, a big desk, a refrigerator, leather couch and chairs. I asked Sully how he got all the stuff. He said the friends you make, and midnight requisitions. Nobody notices they're missing. If it was removed from an office and was going to be put in storage, it would end up in Sully's office."

The Trying Tar Heel Trip

Kopinksy remembers the trying travels of ACC competition during that time.

"We'd hit all the ACC schools—NC State, Duke, North Carolina and Virgina—in one trip during a weekend," he said. "Friday or Sunday, we'd wrestle Virginia on the way up or down. We called it the Tar Heel trip. Wrestling was not as competitive as now in the ACC, so we could wrestle once on Friday, twice on Saturday and once on Sunday."

Second Only to the Ship

When Doyle Royal entered the University of Maryland in 1939, he was a poor boy from Washington, D.C. rich in athletic talent. So when Maryland's tennis coach at the time, Lesley Bopst, offered Royal a job and a room if he enrolled at the school and played tennis for the Terps, Royal didn't hesitate to take the offer.

Royal also played soccer pretty well. His high school, Roosevelt, did not have a soccer team, so he played with a local semiprofessional team. He played soccer at Maryland during his freshman year, then concentrated entirely on tennis. He said soccer "gave him his legs for tennis" and that he preferred playing the racquet sport.

As a tennis player, Royal says he won more than he lost. He was the number one player on the team his senior year. But Royal left his mark at Maryland more as a soccer and tennis coach, roles he served for more than a quarter-century. And in those roles, he won many more then he lost.

As men's soccer coach from 1946 to 1973, Royal fashioned a record of 217 wins, 58 losses and 18 ties. In addition to its numerous appearances in the NCAA title game and its national title in 1968, Maryland dominated conference play under Royal. The Terps won three Southern Conference championships and 15 ACC titles, including ten in a row from 1953 to 1962.

Royal coached dozens of All-Americans, including two-time first-team honorees Jim Belt (1947-48), a center forward, and center halfback Giancarlo Brandoni (1967-68).

"He wasn't a great scorer, but he was a great player," said Royal of Belt. "The ball and him were one and the same. The ball would come to him and it seemed like it could stick to him. He was the best ball handler I've ever coached."

As tennis coach from 1954-1980, Royal coached the Terps to ACC championships in 1957 and 1964 and to six runner-up finishes. His only All-American was left-hander John Lucas in 1976. Lucas also achieved similar honors as a basketball player.

Royal's record as tennis coach was 296-114-1. He amassed an incredible 513 wins in two sports as a Maryland coach, second only Burton Shipley, who coached the men's basketball and baseball teams to 610 wins.Booters Contend for National Titles

The men's soccer team had established a brief time of national superiority prior to their momentous 1968 season. In 1947, The Terps finished the season unbeaten and ranked number one in the country after wins in their last two games over defending national champion Temple, which entered the match with a 19-game winning streak, and previously unbeaten Salisbury Teachers College.

The wins prompted coach Doyle Royal to challenge Springfield College of Massachusetts to play for the national title. But the game never materialized. The only blemish on their record that year was an early-season tie with Loyola.

Maryland's next unbeaten season was in 1958 (9-0-1), but there were no NCAA championships until two years later. The Terps landed in the NCAA championship game in 1960 and 1962, losing both times by one goal to St. Louis University.

In 1960, Maryland had won 33 consecutive regular-season games before losing to Army, 3-1. Cliff Krug then scored eight goals in the last two regular season games as Maryland again qualified for the NCAA tournament.

In Maryland's first game of the tournament against Rutgers, the Terps trailed 3-0 entering the final quarter. Krug, whose 26 goals that season rank first in all-time single-season goals for the Terps, tied the game with 25 second left, and Robert Cummings scored the game winner two minutes into overtime.

Krug scored three goals in a comfortable 4-0 win over Connecticut in a semifinal. Maryland then faced St. Louis, the defending champion, in the final, and Krug scored again to bring the Terps to within one in the third period. But a fourth-period Terps goal was called back for offsides, and Maryland missed its first chance at a national title, losing 3-2.

In 1962, Maryland again qualified for the NCAA tournament despite losing eight starters from the previous year's team. Richard Roe scored both goals, including the game winner in the fourth period, in Maryland's 2-1 season-ending victory over Navy. The Terps entered the NCAA final against St. Louis with a 10-0 record.

Roe scored in the championship match to put Maryland ahead 3-2. But St. Louis scored twice in the final period to win 4-3.

Tournament Tribulations

Maryland also entered the 1968 NCAA title game against Michigan State unbeaten, with 14 wins. Two All-Americans from the previous season, defender Alvaro Bittencourt and goalkeeper Mario Jelencovich, highlighted seven returning starters from the previous season.

Maryland's team featured a strong international flavor. Freshman Melih Sensoy, a defender, is from Turkey. Rocco Morelli was born in Italy but grew up in Brooklyn, and he attended the same junior college as goalkeeper Jelencovich and Giancarlo Brandoni.

"We were mostly Europeans and South Americans," said Morelli. "We had only a couple of Americans. Being from different countries, we wanted to succeed at what we were doing. We lived in Byrd Stadium, so it wasn't too far for us to run up and down the stadium stairs. We used to practice twice a week on our own."

Morelli, a junior college All-American the previous season, lived up to expectations by scoring 15 goals during the regular season.

A key win that season came against Navy in front of 1,000 spectators in College Park in late October. Maryland hadn't beaten

Navy since 1963. It was a typical physical match against Navy. Two Navy players left the field following collisions; one later needed six stitches to close a wound on his face.

Frank Schoon scored the game winner two minutes from the end of the second overtime.

"We played a nice, indirect style of soccer," said Morelli. "We were not very physical, like Navy. The coach was not really involved in the game; he was a nice coach, but he left it to the assistant coaches. Ron Hoch, an assistant, was in the military. He trained us military style with extra running and a lot of physical stuff. Coach Royal just gave us the go-ahead to do it."

In the NCAA tournament, Maryland faced nemesis St. Louis in the first round, and as in 1962, the Billikins were the defending national champions. They were also unbeaten and allowed just five goals all season. But Maryland was also undefeated, was the top ranked team in the nation, and had scored 45 goals in 12 games and recorded four shutouts.

There were 8,500 fans gathered in Byrd Stadium to attend the first NCAA soccer game played in College Park. Maryland won the contest 3-1. One week later, the Terps beat Hartwick 2-1 in a quarterfinal match played in front of 6,500 fans at Byrd Stadium.

Morelli then took over the tournament semifinal against San Jose State in Atlanta in perhaps Maryland's wildest game in NCAA tournament history. Maryland fell behind 2-0 in the first seven minutes. Morelli tied the game in the 15th minute with his second goal. At halftime, Maryland looked like a beaten team. They could muster only five shots, while San Jose State fired 16. The Terps were called offside 10 times.

Morelli tied the game again at three in the third period with a header. And he scored the game winner with a little more than two minutes remaining in the fourth overtime. Had the game ended in a tie after that overtime, San Jose would have advanced due to its 10-1 advantage in corner kicks.

It was the first game Maryland played at night under artificial lights. Maryland's stingy defense had not given up more than two goals in a game all season. Giving up three goals made goal-keeper Mario Jelencovich uncomfortable. He complained his poor eyesight was affected by the lighting in the stadium.

Unhappy Co-Champs

Natural light greeted Maryland when they played the final against Michigan State two days later. But the mood among Maryland's players was dark following the 2-2 tie that left them co-champions. Maryland gave up a goal with 11 minutes remaining in regulation for the tie. Neither team could score in two overtimes, in front of just 826 fans.

The Spartans were able to keep Morelli scoreless. "They triple-teamed me that day," said Morelli. "They kicked the shit out of me. I can still feel where those guys hit me."

In the Maryland locker room after the game, players hung their heads low and talked to themselves about what could have been. "This game was anticlimactic to Thursday night's [game]," said Jalencovich in *The Diamondback*. "After beating a team like San Jose State in a sudden-death overtime, all the excitement was drained out of me."

Still, Jalencovich helped secure Maryland's place as co-champ by stopping two point-blank shots in overtime. He was named the defensive Player of the Tournament.

Maryland advanced to the NCAA semifinals in 1969. It would be 27 years before the Terps again advanced that far in the tournament. Between the appearances, they appeared in the tournament seven times, but did not advance further than the second round. And in 1971, the Terps won the ACC championship for the last time.

13

Jackson Takes Over
Diamond Duties

Maryland baseball's most prolific period during the modern era of Terps athletics stretched from 1965 through 1971. During that time, Maryland won the ACC championship three times and qualified for the NCAA tournament each of those times, all under head coach Elton "Jack" Jackson.

Jackson worked as an assistant coach for Burton Shipley for five seasons after playing five years of minor league baseball. While an undergraduate student at Maryland, Jackson dated a coed in his zoology class. Her father, who was related to Shipley, told Jackson that Shipley wanted him to be Maryland's freshman team coach.

"I worked with him for two weeks, and he said, 'Say, I say, Jack, you and I get along pretty good. Why don't you stay with me and we'll get someone else to work with the freshmen.'"

After he finished his undergraduate studies, Jackson was thinking of leaving Maryland to teach and coach elsewhere. "But Shipley told me that he would coach only one more year and that I had a good chance of getting his job," said Jackson.

Jackson was paid $1,000 a year to be head coach of the baseball team, along with $5,000 to teach physical education. Jackson coached the baseball team through 1990.

No-Hitter, No Win

Jackson had his first winning record four seasons after taking over as skipper in 1961. The next season, 1965, started well, with the Terps winning their first four games, including a 9-0 win over eighth-ranked Maine.

Maryland was 7-2 when it faced South Carolina in the first game of a doubleheader, and the way Jerry Bark was pitching that game, it looked as if the Terps would improve to 8-2. Despite tendonitis in his pitching arm, Bark struck out nine batters and walked only two when he entered the ninth inning. He then struck out the side to preserve a no-hitter, but he couldn't yet take the win because the game went into extra innings tied at 0. It was the second no-hitter in Maryland history. Dick Reitz pitched one against Johns Hopkins in 10-0 win in 1959.

Bark gave up a hit to the leadoff batter in the tenth inning. But Bark and the Terps lasted until the 13th inning, when he gave up a home run on a high fastball and the Terps lost, 1-0.

"It was larceny to lose a game like that," said Jackson in the Diamondback after the game. "We left 12 men on base."

A few weeks later, Bark got the support he needed in a 5-0 win over Virginia in the first game of a doubleheader against the league-leading Cavaliers. Maryland won the second game, 3-1, to clinch its first ACC title with a 10-4 conference record. The Terps did not fare as well in the NCAA East Regional tournament in North Carolina. They lost four games, finishing the season with a 16-8 record.

A Fine Field Fix

Maryland's success in 1965 started with a conversation Jackson had with George Webber, the head of Maryland's physical plant, at a party at the house of golf coach Frank Cronin.

"Webber said, 'Jack, I've done a lot of things for other guys, what can I do for you?' I said, 'George, I want you to bring an engineer out there to measure the slope on the field.'"

Webber discovered the field was five feet lower at 325 feet than it was at home plate. "Balls hit to the outfield would just go," said Jackson. Using dirt dug up from construction of the school's Adult Education Center, Webber's crew regraded the field and placed a new chain-link fence around the field.

Jackson also received help from other Maryland teams. "The track and wrestling teams walked the field with us to pick stones out of the sod," said Jackson. "That's when there really was a of camaraderie. The other coaches were always willing to pull each other along."

Happy Times with Hiser

A big reason for Maryland's success in 1970, the year the Terps won their second ACC title, was Gene Hiser. The Baltimore native was a walk-on who earned All-American honors that year and later played five seasons with the Chicago Cubs.

"He must have weighed 140 pounds soaking wet when he was a freshman," said Jackson. "When he left, he was about 175 pounds and grew eight inches."

Jackson remembers how he converted Hiser from a "Punch and Judy hitter" into a power hitter. "He would hit ground balls and beat them out," said Jackson. "After playing one summer and hitting .390 in a league, he came back to Maryland. About two weeks went by, and I said, 'Gene, you've killed every worm out in front of home plate. You're lunging at the ball constantly.' I took him to the right field area, and we started working on throwing bats."

The exercise helped Hiser open up his hips. "After 15-20 minutes, he said, 'Yeah, I feel that,'" said Jackson. In his next game against Georgetown, Hiser hit home runs in his first two at-bats. "Everybody on the bench said I want to throw bats," said Jackson. Hiser hit 11 home runs the following spring.

Better Late Than Never

When Jackson was an assistant coach to Shipley, he learned a lesson about how to effectively punish tardiness. During a trip south in the late 1950s, the team was scheduled to leave at 8:15 a.m. By departure time, a few players had not shown up.

"Shipley says, 'I say, Bussey, put her in gear,'" said Jackson.

"There were guys banging on the bus to get in and I hear Shipley say, 'I say, Bussey, you keep driving or I'll get another bus driver.' We never had guys late again."

In 1970, Jackson asked his players to meet at 8:00 a.m. to leave for a trip to play Virginia in Charlottesville. "I wanted them in a tie and socks, to look halfway decent," said Jackson. "I look around and there's about five of the guys who didn't have ties or socks. I said, 'You don't go unless you're dressed properly. We're leaving at eight.' They scattered, took off."

Jackson left behind the inadequately dressed players, who later hitched a ride with sports information director Jack Zane. Some of the players were mad at Jackson for leaving the group behind.

During pregame warmups, Jackson, a good friend of the Virginia coach, sat on the Virginia bench. "I said to some of the kids, 'You guys mind if I sit over here? My guys are really ticked at me.' Then 15 minutes before game time, they come running onto the field. We win the game, and I never had any guys late after that."

Maryland clinched the conference title two days later after beating Clemson.

14

Battling the Recruiting Odds

The men's basketball teams endured a phase of mediocrity throughout the 1960s. As the Terps struggled throughout the early 1960s, Millikan fell out of favor with some of the Maryland faithful. Students displayed an effigy with the words "Bud Must Go" in 1963. Some criticized Millikan's preference for plodding play, a slow-down offense supported by a technically sound and aggressive defense.

Dissenters were unhappy with Millikan's inability to recruit top players. Millikan blamed the recruiting woes on insufficient staff.

"Basketball was left behind at Maryland when I coached," he said. "We never had a full-time assistant coach. Many other teams had at least one full-time assistant. Where it hurts you the most is in recruiting. We had a world of people who came and visited Maryland and liked Maryland, but we didn't get enough early contact with them."

Millikan and assistant coach Frank Fellows, who joined the team in 1961, did all recruiting and scouting for the team. Top prospects generally bypassed Maryland for other ACC schools.

In March of that year, university president Dr. Wilson Elkins said Maryland would increase its recruiting in the Maryland-Washington area. He felt recruiting too far from a school's boundaries increased the chance of recruiting scandal.

As a result, Maryland recruited its first black player, John Austin, from DeMatha High School. Austin passed on Maryland, but his teammate, Gary Ward, did sign with the Terps. Ward helped Maryland achieve some success in the mid-1960s.

One highlight stands out during that time. Al Bunge scored 43 points in a game against Yale on January 4, 1960. Today, it ranks as the second most points scored in a game, behind Earnest Graham's 44 against NC State in 1978. Bunge shot 14 of 15 from the floor in the Yale game. "Everything I threw up, went in, hook shots, jumpers, taps, one-hand sets from the corners," said Bunge in the book *Maryland Basketball.* Bunge was a first-team All-ACC selection in 1960.

The Fans Come Back to Cole

When the 1964-65 men's basketball season arrived, Cole Field House had offered little home-court advantage for the Terps. Disappointed with three consecutive losing seasons, fans stayed away. "We played with no fans on the floor," said big man Jerry Greenspan, an All-ACC selection in 1963, in the book *Maryland Basketball.* As far as our opponents were concerned, Cole was a neutral court."

Fans started returning in larger numbers during the 1964-65 season. A strong sophomore class supported that team, including Joe Harrington, a high school All-American from Maine; Jay McMillen, from the backwoods of Pennsylvania; and Gary Williams, a feisty guard from Collingswood, New Jersey.

Williams accepted a scholarship at Maryland over Clemson, Providence and Pittsburgh.

*Gary Williams has had more success at
Maryland as a coach than as a player.*

Maryland finished tied for second in the conference that season and sported an 18-8 record. The other starters on that team, Neil Brayton and Ward, were juniors, so the future looked bright for the basketball team. A loss in the semifinals of the conference tournament to North Carolina State did not quell optimism for the program's immediate future.

Breaking the Basketball Racial Barrier

Billy Jones and Pete Johnson entered Maryland as basketball state champions. Johnson won a state title in Cole Field House with Fairmont Heights High School, about 10 miles from the Maryland campus. Jones did the same at Towson High School of Baltimore.

They were leading scorers on the freshman team in 1964-65. The guards played three years on Maryland's varsity and averaged double figures in scoring.

Johnson ultimately edged Jones in the area of racial legacy. Johnson became the first African American basketball player in the ACC when he joined Maryland's varsity for the 1965-66 season. Jones, also African American, was redshirted that season for academic reasons.

Both players endured racial heckling from fans, most often when Maryland held a lead. And Johnson's appearance in a Maryland uniform served as a prelude for what many consider to be the most profound step made by minorities in college basketball. Maryland hosted the 1966 NCAA Final Four at Cole Field House. Texas Western University, a team of African American players, beat Kentucky in the championship game.

Maryland hosted the 1966 NCAA Final Four at Cole Field House. Texas Western University, a team of African American players, beat Kentucky in the championship game.

From High Hopes to Low Moments

With seven seniors and four juniors on the roster, the Maryland basketball team provided much hope prior to the 1965-66 season A preseason top 20 ranking hyped many to think that Maryland could play in the NCAA final four that would be hosted at the end of the season at Cole Field House.

But it was not to be. Maryland finished the season 14-11 and lost in the first round of the ACC tournament to North Carolina.

The next year, at the end of an 11-14 season, Millikan announced his resignation following a first-round loss to South Carolina in the ACC tournament.

Former players praised Millikan's brilliance, his technical innovations in basketball, and his priority on academics. He worked his players hard, and many appreciated that.

"Everything we did was difficult," said Shue. "On occasion, we would practice three times a day, about two hours each session. You had to do things exactly right. If things weren't going well, we would start running the steps in Ritchie Coliseum. He had drill after drill teaching fundamentals."

When Shue was asked if practices were tedious at times, he laughed. "We used to drag out of there," he said. "It was an important part of life. He was always hard on his players."

Shue said some of Millikan's former players gather each year with the old coach at a golf tournament at Maryland's golf course.

"There wasn't anything I didn't like about him," said Shue, who played 10 years in the NBA and coached 23 years in the league. "Bud was a very dedicated, hard-working, tough, really disciplined coach. That's how he wanted his players to play. He emphasized all the important things. Defense is always your foundation. We were well schooled in executing plays and the fundamentals. When I became a coach, those were the things I emphasized."

Some former players thought his reluctance to adapt to changes in the game helped lead to his downfall as a coach.

"We were sad as hell to see him leave," said guard Billy Jones in *Maryland Basketball*. "His wife was kind of happy he was getting out of it, though. For us, it was very emotional."

When asked if he resigned or was asked to leave, Millikan said it was "50-50. I had been bellyaching for some time to get an assistant. After three or four years of trying, it was hard to be a part of it. I had good times and bad times there." Millikan said the "sorriest time" during his years as Maryland's coach was when he attempted to leave the job during Jim Tatum's reign as athletic director.

"I was actively looking around," he said. "I wanted better recruiting facilities and more pay." An athletic director at a Big Ten school Millikan would not mention had offered him the job as head basketball coach, and Millikan wanted the job. But Millikan says Tatum did not release him from his contract at Maryland.

"It was August, right before football season, and Tatum was on vacation," said Millikan. "He had the football season coming up, and he just didn't want to take the time to hire a basketball coach."

After leaving Maryland, Millikan moved to near Atlanta and opened an office for a company owned by A.V. Williams, one of the founders of the Terrapin Club. He still lives there today. When asked if he looks back at his Maryland years fondly, he says quickly, "Nope, it was just a part of things. I do have many fond memories when I see my former players, though."

Millikan received a pleasant surprise recently when Billy Jones, a member of Millikan's teams from 1965-67, stopped by to visit Millikan at his home. "He came in the door, and chills went up and down my spine," he said.

Millikan cherishes a memory in 1966, when Maryland was playing in Davidson's holiday tournament. Maryland was 4-3 without its top scorer, Jay McMillen, who was out with injury, and faced Davidson in the tournament opener. "The host team always picked what they think is the poorest team in the first round," said Millikan.

Maryland beat Davidson, coached by Lefty Driesell, by one point and beat Army, coached by Bobby Knight, by three points to win the tournament. "I'm probably the only coach in the country who never lost to Lefty and Bobby Knight," said Millikan.

After leaving Maryland following 17 years as head coach, Millikan never coached basketball again.

Camp Kehoe

Frank Costello, one of the top high school high jumpers in the country, was all set to sign with the University of Michigan, until he—and his parents—met Jim Kehoe.

Costello initially favored Michigan because its track coach, Don Canham, was an NCAA high jump champion in 1940. The week he had planned to visit Michigan, Kehoe called and asked Costello to visit the College Park campus. After meeting the legendary Kehoe during a one-day visit, Costello cancelled his trip to Michigan.

"I fell in love with Kehoe," said Costello.

Their special relationship produced one of Maryland's most successful track athletes and coaches and a father-son type of bond that continues today. Costello, along with long jumper Mike Cole, became Maryland's first track and field sole NCAA champions in 1965, three years after John Belitza tied for the NCAA pole vault championship in 1962. He also was head track coach from 1974 to 1980, during a time when Maryland received its highest national ranking.

Costello opted for Maryland despite a less than elaborate recruiting trip. "I couldn't get anybody if I recruited like that," said Costello. "When I recruited, you had to wine and dine them."

Costello and his parents met Kehoe at a Dairy Queen near College Park. Kehoe first talked to Costello's parents alone and then to Costello. Later, they walked around the campus. Costello never met any of Maryland's other track athletes.

"He was a little intimidating at the time," said Costello of Kehoe. "I wasn't used to a guy like him. I was a bit apprehensive. And I had never been more south than South Jersey. Kehoe recruited the parents; he didn't recruit the kid. That's how he recruited, and that's the type of person he recruited, too. He knew it didn't really matter what I thought. It didn't matter to me. I thought, 'Hey, Maryland sounds cool, I'll go there.' It was an easy decision. I knew from a track point of view it was a good place to go."

Kehoe, the former army officer, tried to run a military-type operation with his track team. Once a week, Kehoe inspected beds at Ritchie Coliseum, prompting some of the guys to stage a lookout.

"There would be mass panic," said Costello. "You better not have a *Playboy* [magazine] laying around. You look back on it, and it was unbelievable."

Dick Dull, an All-ACC javelin thrower and future Maryland athletic director, worked as a dorm monitor for Kehoe. "The floor had better been clean," he said. "It was truly out of boot camp."

Curfews were strictly enforced on trips and in the dormitories. If Kehoe discovered an athlete missing curfew on a trip, the athlete had to find another place to sleep. "We stayed in large dormitories, which made it difficult to sneak in," said Costello. "If a guy came in late, we all knew it, and the coach was there. I've seen him tell guys, 'Here's when your race starts tomorrow, one o'clock, you better be there. Where you are between now and then, I couldn't care less, get out of here,'" said Costello. "And he'd said, 'Find your own way home, too, after the race.' We'd all just sit there and chuckle to death. I heard one guy slept in a fraternity one night."

In the dorms, Ritchie Coliseum and Byrd Stadium, one athlete was in charge of making sure the others did not break curfew.

At the Byrd Stadium rooms, that responsibility fell to Dull. Kehoe made sure Dull played no favorites.

"I had five or six teammates who would constantly go out drinking on weekends and throw it in my face," said Dull, with a laugh. "When I went to tell Kehoe, I told him only about one. Kehoe said, 'Young fella, he's not drinking alone.' By the time I left the room, he got all seven names out of me. And Frank was one of them."

Sorry, Dad, Thought You Were Watching

Costello won the NCAA indoor and outdoor titles as a sophomore, the first year he was eligible for varsity competition. A one-week span that year provided his most fond competitive memories at Maryland.

His first jump cleared seven feet when he won the IC4A indoor meet in New York at Madison Square Garden, in front of family and friends.

The following week, Costello won his first national title at the NCAA indoor championships in Detroit's Cobo Arena. The meet appeared live on national television. Costello was battling John Rambo from Long Beach State, a 1964 Olympic bronze medalist, in a sudden-death jump-off. Both had cleared 6'11", but missed at seven feet. The remaining spectators gathered down at the end of the track where the event was taking place.

"People didn't leave, and they were tearing down the end of the track, it was just us jumping," he said.

In the jump-off, both competitors attempted to clear the same height. If they were both successful, the bar was raised an inch. If they both missed, the bar was lowered an inch. After four rounds between 6'11" and 7'1", the bar was set at 6'11". Rambo, jumping first, missed. When Costello cleared, he won his first NCAA championship.

"The whole thing took an hour," said Costello. "But it was my best day competing. I was young and scared, but as it went on, I gained more confidence. I didn't think I was going to win the national championship."

Caught up in the moment, Costello thought the completion of his event was broadcast on television. But the broadcast ended before the high jump had been completed. Costello says as the announcers signed off, they mentioned the jump-off between himself and Rambo.

Costello's father was sitting by the telephone waiting to hear from his son. "I didn't call home for two hours," said Costello. "I call him, one ring, he picks it up, and he said, 'Who won, who won?'"

Keeping Pace with Kehoe

Costello's older teammates offered one bit of advice to the freshman as he prepared to travel with a few elite members of the team to New York for a meet his freshman year. They told Costello to stay close to Kehoe, because "when the door opens up, he's on his way," he said.

When train door opened up in New York City, the race began. "This guy could walk faster than any human being. He had the biggest stride. I was knocking people over trying to stay with him. He never said a word until we got in a cab."

Once in the cab, the intensity continued. "The cab driver's driving like an idiot and the whole time Coach was in the front seat just staring at him. He says, 'Son, you're going to have a short life if you keep driving like this.' He paid the guy, gave him a tip, and said, 'Let me tell you something, the best thing about New York is leaving!'"

The World Beater

When Frank Costello was laying the groundwork for building a national-class track and field program in College Park in the mid-1970s, the most heralded athlete that would ever wear the Terp thinclads was developing into a fine athlete about 200 miles away in a northern New Jersey city.

Costello grew up in the city of Elizabeth, about 20 minutes away from Renaldo Nehemiah's hometown of Scotch Plains. He first saw Nehemiah compete as a sophomore in high school. Costello knew he had a good chance of signing Nehemiah to attend Maryland.

"I already had [Greg] 'Fly' Robertson, a really good hurdler, and that helped," said Costello. He said Nehemiah had told him he wanted to attend Maryland, but Nehemiah had not yet made a decision. Costello's anxiety increased when he called Nehemiah on a Friday evening and discovered he was not home. Costello called his brother David, then a high school track coach in New Jersey, and found out that Nehemiah was visiting USC.

"I was a wreck all weekend," he said.

Nehemiah had traveled west to visit USC and UCLA, mostly, he said, to satisfy parental pressures and because of the reputation of their athletic programs. However, one other school was on the top of Nehemiah's list. Nehemiah said he was enthralled by the "impeccable" facilities at the University of Tennessee, one of the top collegiate track programs in the country. "And after seeing the campus, all I could think about was bright orange [the school color]."

Nehemiah wanted to attend Tennessee, but as he remembers, the only scholarship they could offer that season went to long jumper Jason Grimes. "They said they thought I would burn out," he said. "I'm still bitter to this day about that."

With Tennessee out of the picture, it came down to Maryland and either USC or UCLA. During his USC trip, Nehemiah says the school provided him a female escort who just happened to be Miss Hawaii. "I had never been around a woman that beautiful," he said.

Renaldo Nehemiah

UCLA track officials told Nehemiah during his visit that he would never be anything unless he went to a West Coast school. "I didn't like their arrogance," he said. Nehemiah said his visit to Maryland "was the most fun. It was a city unto itself and was a great track school at that time. And I met a girl, but on my own." While Costello fretted during Nehemiah's trip west, the hurdler knew on the flight back to New Jersey that he would attend Maryland. He told Costello of his intent to attend Maryland when the coach finally reached Nehemiah by phone that Sunday night. Still, Costello took no chances.

"I called up [assistant coach] Dick Dull and said, let's go," said Costello. "We drove up to New Jersey and signed him that night."

"When we walked out of the house, Frank turned to me and said, 'Dick, do you realize what we just did here?'" said Dull. "Frank did, but I didn't." Neither did athletic director Jim Kehoe. "I told Kehoe that I just signed the greatest track and field athlete that the University of Maryland will ever see," said Costello. "He said, good, good, glad to hear it."

Nehemiah ran 12.9 hand-timed in the high school high hurdles. He was the first high schooler to run the event in under 13 seconds. In the summer following Nehemiah's senior year of high school, he ran the college-level hurdles for the first time during a USA vs. Russia junior track meet. The college hurdles are three inches higher than the high school hurdles and are the standard level for the highest international competition. Nehemiah finished in a world junior record, which he set for the last time in 1978 in 13.23.

"Coach Kehoe gets on the phone and says, 'Good God, it says this guy is going to Maryland,'" said Costello. "I said, 'Coach, this is the guy I was telling you about.' He said, 'Oh, I didn't know he was that good.'"

Nehemiah entered Maryland thinking he could be the best hurdler in the world his freshman year. But after finishing second and third, respectively, in his first two races, he felt far from superior. "I put a lot of pressure on myself," he said. In one of those races at the CYO Invitational in Cole Field House, Nehemiah finished third. He said he briefly thought about quitting track if he lost another race.

But that thought was made irrelevant when Nehemiah won his next race at an indoor meet in Philadelphia. His next win at a meet in New York City was more emphatic. Nehemiah set his first world record of 7.07 in the 60-meter hurdles at the Millrose Games. It was the first of 13 high hurdle world records Nehemiah set running for Maryland.

During the following outdoor season, Nehemiah finished second in the high hurdlers at the NCAA meet, losing by .01 of a second to Greg Foster of UCLA. It was Nehemiah's only loss that year, and for good reason. "I had just run the anchor leg of the four-by-100-meter relay," he said. "I had 15 minutes before the start of the hurdles race. I could barely catch my breath."

The following week, with no relay event to worry about, Nehemiah beat Foster to win the high hurdles at the U.S. National outdoor championships. He finished the season ranked number one in the world.

Maryland had its strongest representation of All-Americans that season. Seven athletes earned the coveted honors, including Brian Melley in the high jump (second), Bob Calhoun(who grew up as a neighbor of Nehemiah's in New Jersey) in the long jump (third), Greg Robertson in the 55-meter high hurdles (third) and Ian Pyka in the shot put (sixth).

Before his sophomore season, Nehemiah made a pledge to be, as he said, "number one, the most dominant, and the fastest." He fulfilled all of his own expectations.

It started with setting three indoor world records in eight days at meets in Toronto, Philadelphia and New York. Later that indoor season, he won the high hurdles at the NCAA indoor meet for the second consecutive year. He also won the event at the NCAA outdoor championships for the first time later that year after setting the outdoor world record for the first time at an invitational meet in California. But it was a surreal performance at the Penn Relays in Philadelphia that spring that prompts track fans to still shake their heads in bewilderment when they reflect on that performance.

"Still today, people say to me they can't believe what I did," he said. Nehemiah's Remarkable Relay Runs took place on two days in late April at Philadelphia's Franklin Field in 1978. A glorious sunny spring day with a cool breeze greeted all at the Franklin Field for the final day of the three-day meet. A capacity crowd of 40,000 helped provide a profound backdrop for one of the most dynamic days of college track and field.

Early in the afternoon, Nehemiah had already anchored the shuttle hurdle relay to a win, avenging a disqualification after winning the event the previous year.

In the 4x200-meter relay final, Nehemiah anchored the team and received the baton in third place, 10 meters behind the leader. Closing a 10-meter deficit in a 200-meter race is considered a fairly impossible mission. Nehamiah ran the anchor leg in 19.4 seconds, winning at the tape. The world record at the time was 19.83. Many of crowd, including myself, were stunned to a moment of bewilderment following the win.

The 4x400-meter relay is scheduled as the last event of big meets. Running a 400-meter race well requires speed, strength, control and discipline. Add guts to all those qualities, and you've got the ideal quarter-miler.

Despite Nehemiah's evident attributes, what he faced as he took the baton for his anchor leg seemed even impossible for world record holder Michael Johnson.

Nehemiah said he was "pissed" because Maryland's lead leg struggled to finish in about 50 seconds, well below his best. He said that anger propelled him to a fast start.

"I ran about 85 percent to the first turn," said Nehemiah. "I had the advantage of more top end speed than the other guys, so I can cover more ground working that hard. On the back stretch, I needed to make a move to get closer."

As Nehemiah completed the backstretch, he was in fourth place. He had made up about 15 meters on the leader by that point of the race. It seemed the entire crowd rose to its feet, creating a surreal sound of expectant glee. "When I got to the 200, I said I was going to kick," he said. "If I die, that's okay."

As he came off the last turn, he was six meters behind the leader, Tim Dale of Villanova. "I ran through a lot of pain," he said. "I felt it in the race. The crowd was yelling and screaming. I squinted my eyes and could see in front of me, but they weren't really open. I just had to see if I could catch him."

Nehemiah won by a few meters. "I may have run two more steps and then collapsed," he said. "It was a painful memory," he said. "But I revel at the impression those races left on people."

An Unsettling Year

Nehemiah's junior season started strongly. But an admittedly immature mistake led to misfortune that was a prelude to a troubling outdoor season.

In between the indoor and outdoor season, Nehemiah sprained his ankle while playing a pickup basketball game in the football building gymnasium. The injury placed him in a cast, and he missed weeks of training. Nehemiah avoided the wrath of Coach Costello by telling him he turned the ankle running on the school's golf course.

But he couldn't avoid a different confrontation a few weeks later. During his down time, Nehemiah traveled to Germany to meet with representatives from Puma. He was troubled by an NCAA rule that prevented him from keeping money he was offered to compete in meets in Europe during the indoor and outdoor seasons. International amateur rules, however, allowed him to place the money in a trust fund to be used for competing expenses, so long as he was not part of a college team.

Puma offered Nehemiah $125,000 to sign an endorsement deal. He quickly accepted the offer. Nehemiah later caused a stir when he competed for a local club track team at the outdoor Kansas Relays the same day the Maryland team competed at the outdoor ACC meet and didn't win it for the first time in 26 years.

The 1980 outdoor season was not a fun one for the Maryland track team. With Nehemiah suddenly gone from the team, the team's collective broad shoulders began to slump. The swagger of the previous few seasons had been replaced with a bewildered shuffle. Maryland dealt with false claims of racial discord. The team's spiritual leader the previous few years, Greg "Fly" Robertson, had graduated the year before. Other colorful characters, as well as prominent performers, had gone as well, such as nationally ranked shot putter Ian Pyka.

After the disheartening second-place finish at the ACC meet, the team rallied a month later to win the more competitive IC4A meet, the unofficial championship of the East Coast. It would be Costello's last great triumph as Maryland's head track coach. The previous December, he had announced his resignation as head coach, effective following the season. He left behind six years of conference dominance and mostly fond memories of helping develop one of the greatest athletes in the history of Maryland's athletic program.

16

The Growth of Women's Athletics

Teams Thrive on Frugality in the '60s and '70s

The challenges experienced by women's sports in the 1960s helped lay the foundation for the passage of Title IX legislation the following decade. Their struggles were laced with innocent enthusiasm and an embracing of adventure. Their experiences were similar to the ones shared by Maryland's men's teams during the initial evolution of their sports a half-century earlier.

A McKnight in Shining Armor

In her first year as head coach of the first officially recognized Maryland women's basketball team in 1971, Dottie McKnight led the Lady Terps to a 12-2 record. By the time she stepped down as head coach after four seasons with a 44-17 record, Maryland had won two state championships.

It's no surprise the women's team enjoyed immediate success. They had been playing the sport at Maryland in various forms since the early 1900s. McKnight coached a team that played other colleges since 1965, along with the field hockey team.

At that time, Maryland also fielded women's teams in tennis and swimming, but they weren't administered or funded by the school's athletic department. Instead, the Women's Athletic Association, which was part of the school's intramural program, administered the teams, and the school's college of Physical Education, Health and Recreation funded the teams, as did cake sales and cookie sales and car washes, along with donations from the athletes and coaches, who received no salaries. Most coaches, if not all, worked at the school in another capacity.

"We would do whatever we could to make the money," said Dr. Joanne Holt, a Professor Emerita in kinesiology at Maryland who started coaching women's teams in 1968. "What we did is beg, borrow and steal. Sometimes we took money out of student activity fees via intramurals."

Tennis Travels

Holt coached the tennis team and remembers some adventures that showed the spunk and savvy required to maintain women's teams at that time.

Holt says it was difficult for the girls to get prolonged rest during a six-hour car ride to Albany, New York for a competition. That's because they continuously had to search for coins—out of their pockets, mostly—to pay numerous tolls.

During that trip, Holt admits she was driving too fast and was pulled over by a police officer. The team captain sitting in the front seat, Linda Kukowski, showed a strong sense of leadership and offered to negotiate with the officer.

"She said, 'Let me talk to the cop,'" said Holt, with a laugh. "So she and another girl get out as the cop is walking to the car. They start talking to him and showed the officer their white tennis outfits. The other girls in the car are laughing pretty hard. The girls said if he gave me a ticket, the team would have to go back home. They said I would have to pay the fine myself and that I'm not getting paid for this, and if I get the ticket I won't be able to go with them on the trip to Princeton the next weekend. Then the cop walks up and says, 'This is a warning.'"

McKnight came to Maryland after teaching and coaching at Michigan State, where women's teams traveled in buses. When McKnight started coaching at Maryland, the team often traveled in cars owned by students.

During one trip to play George Washington University's basketball team in downtown D.C., one of the cars broke down on a major street. The team pushed the car into a nearby gas station, then piled into Coach McKnight's car.

"We had at least eight people in my car; it was more than legal, that's for sure," said McKnight. "That was pretty nerve-wracking." The team relaxed well enough to win the game. Afterward, they picked up the student's car at the gas station and drove back to school in relative comfort.

She Goes Strong to the Washing Machine

During a three-day tournament in Princeton, Holt's tennis team faced an equipment dilemma that caught them by surprise. No player brought more than one white outfit because Holt said they all expected to lose their first match.

After three players won their first matches and another player won her second match, their teammates pitched in to wash their uniforms at a nearby laundromat. "We were going to the laundromat all the time," said Holt. "The next year, we got white sweats."

Feed Me, and You're a Sponsor

The female athletes of the '60s showed a frugal spirit out of necessity. Dr. Holt, who coached several women's sports at a small private college in Minnesota before arriving at Maryland, remembers how one of her tennis players saved her three-dollar meal money on trips and instead ate food off the plates of her team-mates.

Some pleaded poverty to workers in food stores and walked out with free fruit. "They talked about it being a donation to the program," said Holt. "They told [the store workers] that they'd put their names in our tennis magazine as being a donor for the program. We didn't have a tennis magazine. [The Maryland girls] were a lot more creative than my Minnesota kids."

Holt says the school paid for 45 kilts to be shared as uniform bottoms for all members of the volleyball, basketball, lacrosse, tennis and field hockey teams. Events were often scheduled to ensure all the teams had enough kilts to wear. The girls had to buy their own undergarments, and many colored the white garments red to make themselves less conspicuous during a fall or if they fell victim of a gust of wind.

Holt remembers how one year some of her tennis players wore shorts donated by the men's soccer team. "The top players, most of them had money and didn't have to worry about it," said Holt. "But for other players, that was the only way they could wear a team uniform."

The Woeful Ward Years

In 1967, led by first-year coach Bob Ward, a former all-American for the Terps, the Maryland football team ended the season winless, the first time that happened since the team first played in 1892. The next season, Ward won only two games. When Maryland beat North Carolina in 1968, ending a 16-game losing streak, Ward called it the greatest day of his life.

The players called for Ward to resign, claiming he took scholarships away, hit players during practice, and did not try to understand their problems. Ward denied the allegations.

Maryland's athletic department was on unstable footing when the controversy unraveled. Athletic director William Colby had retired, and his successor, former Maryland track star and coach Jim Kehoe, was waiting for Colby to leave office. "I wasn't prepared to handle such an incident so quickly," he said in the book *The Terrapins: Maryland Football*. "We were in deep, deep trouble. Major teams were performing badly and we were in trouble financially."

Kehoe called a meeting of the football players to voice their troubles. Kehoe and Ward attended the meeting. A day later, Ward resigned. Kehoe thought Ward's ambitions cost him the job. "I never met a man who wanted to win more desperately and worked harder at it than him," he said in the book *The Terrapins: Maryland Football.* "This could have been the problem."

Kehoe fired one of his best friends from a position he loved. One media report said Kehoe walked quietly and alone through the concourse of Cole Field House, back to his office, tears forming in his eyes.

Lows with Lester

Kehoe said he picked Roy Lester as the next football head coach because he had the ability to get along with the youngsters and heal the wounds on the team. He also said the new coach had to offer "good guidance and direction" to young players and be a winner. Lester was an assistant coach under Tommy Mont and a highly successful local high school head coach.

But Lester had little to work wit,h and after just seven wins in three losing seasons, Kehoe reluctantly fired him to "get football built so it would bring in some money." Attendance at home games was starting to dwindle. In three successive home games during the 1970 season, the largest crowd was 18,200.

Lester said he could have turned the program around if he was given the chance. He did, however, leave the next coach, Jerry Claiborne, with a strong recruiting class. And Claiborne used that group to achieve near immediate success.

So Be It

If Curley Byrd is the father of Maryland athletics, then Jim Kehoe certainly is the school's most shining son.

Kehoe devoted close to half of his life to Maryland as a star track athlete, the most dominating track and field and cross-country coach in the history of the ACC, and the school's most successful athletic director.

His fire 'em up, keep-it-shipshape style inspired many but also riled others. If you knew Jim Kehoe—even if you didn't agree with him—it was difficult to dislike him. And it was easy to admire him. He talked a grand but simple game, but he also backed it up with a maniacal work ethic and a charismatic style.

What Once Was

Jim Kehoe was an aimless youth until he met Dr. Philip Bird Hopkins, his track coach at Bel Air High School in Maryland. Hopkins taught Kehoe the values of hard work and study. Until then, Kehoe had little ambition for college or to compete in athletics.

He used running in high school to improve his speed for tennis, his sport of preference at the time, and soccer. But all that changed after a one-mile race that he entered simply to set a strong pace so that a teammate could set a record. He led after the half-mile and felt so good that he kept going, winning by a comfortable margin.

By the time Kehoe graduated from Maryland in 1940, he ran the half-mile in 1:50.7, a time that was not bettered at Maryland for 23 years. Kehoe was the indoor and outdoor 880-yard Southern Conference champion in 1940.

Typical of athletes during that time period, Kehoe's scholarship came from making money as a dorm cleaner and a food server at the dining hall to help pay for school. Kehoe met his wife Barbara while serving her dinner.

"He brought me all the ice cream I wanted," said Barbara Kehoe. The Kehoes live in quaint home in quiet and rural Chesapeake Beach, near the central western shore of the Chesapeake Bay. Children and grandchildren stay at a house the Kehoes own across the street when they visit. Pictures of Kehoe the runner, coach and athletic administrator take up nearly every space on the walls in the hallway of the house. They are reminders of a time in his life far more hectic than the one he has lived in peaceful retirement

It's impossible for a proud man like Jim Kehoe, who has accomplished so much in a lifetime, to stray far from the things that remind him of what he has achieved. As a coach, Kehoe's team won 15 ACC indoor track titles, 15 ACC outdoor track titles and eight ACC cross-country titles.

Dozens of scrapbooks contain letters that remind him of his work as an athletic director; hundreds of pictures and newspapers clippings recount his action as an athletic administrator and his conquests as an elite athlete and coach. Even at the age of 85, Jim Kehoe is still about what once was at the University of Maryland.

Running a Tight Ship

The only thing that seemed more important to Kehoe than a commitment to Maryland athletics was a commitment to a moralistic lifestyle. He has never drunk alcohol, nor has he ever smoked. Kehoe, the former army commander, felt it was his mission to make life better for the young people of America.

Early in his tenure as athletic director, he told the school newspaper, the *Diamondback*, "How any sane person can read the paper, watch TV, know what's going on in the area of morals, drugs and alcoholism and not be devoting every spare minute of their time and try and alleviate it is something I cannot and never will understand."

This excerpt from a story in the *Diamondback* about Kehoe speaks volumes about the man's impact. "Fifty years ago, as the story goes, God created Jim Kehoe in the image of himself. And while it can't be said the world has changed significantly, Kehoe has been a pretty fair public relations man for the virtues of hard work, high morals, and patriotism."

Kehoe would not allow the musical *Hair* to be performed in Cole Field House, home arena of the men's and women's basketball teams, despite the fact that a nude scene was taken out.

"I am opposed to any show that would present men and women unclothed or in the nude," he told the *Diamondback*. "I don't believe it's in the students' best interest."

Kehoe had more serious matters than partially nude musicals to consider when he took over as athletic director. There were the struggles of the football and basketball teams, the only revenue-producing sports for the entire athletic department. ACC basketball teams reached the NCAA final four six times in the 1960s. Maryland was not one of them. North Carolina's four ACC schools—Duke, North Carolina State, North Carolina and Wake Forest—had won 15 of the 16 ACC basketball championships.

In 1967, ACC football teams attracted more than one million spectators for the first time. And female athletes at Maryland were pressuring the school for official recognition of their sports.

During a visit to his home in April 2003, Kehoe would not confirm that Maryland's athletic department was operating a deficit when he took over as athletic director. But reports about Kehoe leaving his post as athletic director in the *Washington Post* in 1978 made reference to deficits up to $170,000.

Despite the poor performances of its football and basketball teams, most of Maryland's teams still dominated the Atlantic Coast Conference, due to the success of its non-revenue sports. Maryland's athletic department won the Carmichael Cup, given to the school whose teams performed the best overall in the conference, five times in its first seven years, including the inaugural season in 1961-62

The Right Hires Help Sell Tickets

Maryland's president Dr. Wilson Elkins said he picked Kehoe as athletic director because of his familiarity with the athletic program and the fact that he recognized improvements needed to be made in football and basketball.

Four days after accepting the position, Kehoe said his job was having the right people doing the right job. Aside from Fellows, early Kehoe hires helped build the admired legacy of Maryland athletics of the 1970s. They included Jerry Claiborne as new football coach; Lefty Driesell as new basketball coach; Chris Weller as the women's basketball coach; Tom Fields as head of the Maryland Educational Foundation, the fundraising arm of the department; and Jack Zane as the director of sports information.

Kehoe made recruiting top athletes a priority when he took office. "We need to reach a point where every one our athletes feels the way we do about the program," he said in the *Washington Daily News*. "Our best recruiters then will be former athletes."

In Kehoe's first two years in office, basketball season tickets increased from 225 to 3000 and football season tickets increased 50 percent to 7500.

Sacrifice Fly

Jack Zane worked in Maryland's athletic office off and on for half a century. He was an assistant to sports information director Joe Blair from 1955 to 1962, then returned to work as SID in 1969. Zane also worked in Maryland's ticket office and later directed the formation of the Terrapin Wall of Fame area in the Comcast Center before retiring in 2003.

While keeping score of a Terps baseball game, Zane noticed a center fielder sprinting toward the dugout in the middle of an inning. The center fielder was trying to get out of the way of a small plane, which would normally have landed in College Park airport about two miles away. But the plane was trying to make an emergency landing in the football practice field, which connected to the baseball outfield.

The plane stopped abruptly after hitting a fence on the far side of the practice field, its nose digging firmly into the ground. Zane sensed an opportunity to advance his journalism career. He ran over to a nearby pay phone and called his fraternity house and convinced a brother to deliver Zane's camera and film up to the baseball field. Zane sold the picture to the *Washington Post* and the Associated Press.

Zane remembers that no one was hurt in the accident.

Nearly Missed Namath?

Moses Malone was not the only "Big One that Got Away."

Joe Namath, the future Hall of Fame quarterback for the New York Jets, wanted to play football at Maryland. But after he scored below 800 on his college entrance exam, Maryland could not take him. Maryland was bound to the 800 rule, which required all ACC schools to refuse admission to any athlete who did not reach that number on the exam.

To ensure the Terps would not compete against Namath, the Terps did the next best thing to playing him—NOT playing against him. Maryland head coach Tom Nugent told assistant coach Bernie Reed to find Namath a scholarship at a school that would not play Maryland.

"He called Georgia first, then he called Alabama and talked to the Bear [Bryant, former Maryland football coach]," said Jack Zane, longtime Maryland sports information director. "Bryant had one scholarship left. He said, yeah, I'll take him." Namath became an All-American at Alabama.

Lefty's Legacy

It was a familiar scene, but a different setting. With the crowd roaring, Lefty Driesell walked onto the court at a Maryland basketball game and flashed the familiar victory sign atop his right hand pointing to the rafters. This time, he strode more deliberately. And this was not the cavernous Cole Field House, but the cacophonous Comcast Center, Maryland basketball's new arena.

A smiling female cheerleader held each of his arms, providing perhaps the most glamorous on-court escort of his 41-year coaching career. This time, for Lefty, there was no game to be played, but the crowd did not care. They cheered for the legacy of Lefty Driesell, a legacy conceived in College Park 33 years earlier and celebrated for one last time during halftime of a home game against ACC conference rival NC State on January 30, 2003.

The fans stood and cheered for two minutes. Twice Driesell responded by raising his arm in the symbolic "V." Lefty's bold, quick-paced walks onto the court of Cole typified the swagger of Maryland basketball during that era. But this time, there was no bravado, just much to savor.

The left-hander was back on the College Park campus for only the second time since 1986, when he departed as Maryland's

Lefty Driesell

basketball coach amid the fallout from the death of Len Bias. The previous summer, Driesell appeared on campus for his induction into the Maryland Athletic Hall of Fame.

Driesell's high-profile athletic career began in Norfolk, Virginia, where he won a state championship with the basketball team at Granby High School. At Duke, he played in the first ACC tournament in 1954 and on a 10th-ranked team his senior year.

As a high school coach, he won a city title at Granby and a state title later at Newport News High School. Driesell established his reputation for a tireless work ethic and renown for recruiting during his first college coaching job at Davidson. While recruiting the son of former Terp player Fred Hetzel, he let a snake run up and down his arm. It was enough to persuade the younger Hetzel to bypass Maryland for Davidson.

Minutes before the ceremony in his honor began at the Comcast Center, Driesell sat at floor level behind one of the baskets, waiting for his cue to walk onto the court. Kehoe sat quietly and proudly to the left of Lefty. When Kehoe hired Driesell in 1969, it was one of the more profound personnel moves in the history of college athletics. Jim Kehoe was as determined as Driesell was dynamic, and the duo helped propel University of Maryland to the forefront of collegiate athletics.

During the Driesell ceremony, the 85-year-old Kehoe managed to flash the same flair that symbolized his nine years as athletic director. Kehoe was known for a dapper dressing style. He often wore bright and bold-colored plaid sports jackets, and tonight his brazen attire boasted of a special significance

"I wore this same outfit when I first met Lefty," said Kehoe, wearing brown wingtip shoes, a tan turtleneck shirt and a royal blue, white and red plaid jacket. They met on a late February weekend in 1969. Kehoe was in North Carolina leading the Maryland track team in the ACC indoor championships. He took time to meet with Driesell, then the head coach at Davidson.

Kehoe considered only one other man for Maryland's basketball coach, DeMatha High School head coach Morgan Wooten.

In late winter, 1969, Driesell and Davidson lost in the NCAA Eastern Regional final to North Carolina on a last-second shot by Charley Scott. After the game, Kehoe invited Driesell and his wife over to his house to talk about coaching at Maryland.

"He had been talking to me a great deal," said Driesell. "I wasn't interested in leaving Davidson. He said, 'We'll have Vince Lombardi in the fall [coaching the Washington Redskins], Ted Williams in the spring [coaching the Washington Senators] and you in the winter.'"

Kehoe told Dreisell he had to make up his mind that evening or he would offer the job to Morgan Wooten. Kehoe then directed Driesell and his wife to go into a nearby room to discuss the offer. After a brief discussion with his wife, Driesell decided to take the job.

"He's a good salesman," Driesell said of Kehoe. "That's the way you do it." Lefty had said he would retire if he won the NCAA championship. A few weeks before being honored at the Comcast Center, Driesell announced his retirement from college coaching without having won the big one. But that doesn't mean he is not a champion.

The UCLA of the East

While coaching Davidson at the NCAA Eastern Regional at Cole Field House, Driesell had breakfast with former Maryland players Joe Harrington and Jay McMillen as well as Jack Heise, a former Terp basketball manager and a loyal fan. McMillen said he could see Maryland basketball as UCLA is on the West Coast. They both are located in a metropolitan area and play in a big-time conference.

Driesell used the phrase at the press conference that announced he was taking the job, and the media translated that into Maryland's new objective to become "the UCLA of the East." From that point, Maryland basketball was on a quest to emulate the many-times national champion from Los Angeles.

Long Hours

To become the head coach at Maryland in 1969, Driesell had left the security of a Davidson program that sported a 27-3 record and returned several prominent players. He signed with Maryland for a reported $21,000 annual salary, the use of a courtesy car and a summer basketball camp at Cole Field House. He was afforded the maximum number of scholarships the conference allowed.

Driesell worked 18-hour days and expected the same from his assistants, who included Harrington and George Raveling, who also coached the freshman team. Driesell renovated the basketball training rooms, offices, and locker rooms, where he added framed pictures of the players and motivational signs.

During his first season, with the help of Maryland's promotions director Russ Potts, he started a weekly television show, and all games were broadcast on radio. Seven home games were televised the next season. He supported recruiting with newspaper advertisements.

Cole Field House also became a more intimate and intimidating place when Driesell took over. Floor seats were installed, the pep band played "Hail to the Chief" as Driesell walked onto the floor, and large crowds returned to the arena.

The work was not all fun for Driesell. "I would never do that again, go to a school as low as Maryland was," he said in the book *Maryland Basketball*. "Life is too short. I feel too old right now to work that hard again."

Lifting Maryland's Spirits

Driesell's first two years ended 13-13 and 14-12, respectively. Players had a tough time adjusting from Fellows's instructional approach to Driesell's in-your-face style. Practices were longer and more grueling. One player complained that Driesell shouted much more than Fellows did.

Will Hetzel, a forward during Fellows's last year, struggled to adjust to Driesell's style. He was injured during a loose ball drill and later began Driesell's first season on the bench.

But Hetzel persevered, and he prompted the first wild celebration of an ACC victory at Cole. After his 40-footer at the buzzer beat Duke, 52-50, the crowd stormed the court and carried Driesell, flashing the V-sign, around the floor. And for the first time, the pep band played the song "Amen," a tradition that continues after Terp home victories.

Landing the Big Ones

Lefty Driesell's impressive recruiting complemented increased interest in the program. His freshman team during the 1970-71 season, which included Jim O'Brien and Howard White, finished the year 16-0 and ranked number one in the country. They were his first recruiting class.

Lefty called White "an Alcindor of the backcourt," a reference to the great center Lew Alcindor, who later changed his name to Kareem Abdul-Jabbar.

Driesell reportedly told White, "After we win the national title, you and I will be riding down Pennsylvania Avenue with President Nixon and people will point and say, 'Hey, who's that man riding with Howard White and Lefty?'"

Maryland's second freshman basketball team included Len Elmore, from undefeated Power Memorial High School in New York City, and Tom McMillen, the brother of former Terp player Jay and the first high school basketball player to have his jersey retired to the Basketball Hall of Fame.

Gamecock Fights

Three intense games with South Carolina highlighted Driesell's second season as coach. The first game at Columbia, South Carolina ended with more than four minutes remaining and South Carolina ahead 96-70. A fight was started after South Carolina's John Ribock punched Driesell.

"It was like a riot," said Driesell. "One of their players had one of my players on the ground, and I tried to separate them. That's when Ribock hit me. [South Carolina coach] Frank McGuire said I must have been mistaken and that I hit myself. I said, 'Wait till they come back to Cole Field House, we'll get them.'"

Much interest surrounded the rematch about three weeks later in Cole Field House. Kehoe said Maryland could have sold 50,000 tickets to the game against the number two Gamecocks.

Before the game, Driesell warned South Carolina players to be aware of spectators charging the court. South Carolina coach Frank McGuire threatened that his team might not make the trip. The ACC said any player who fought during the game would be suspended for the season.

"Students were dressed like militia," said Driesell. "It was great."

Maryland held the ball for long stretches and led 4-3 at half-time. "They just didn't play us," said Driesell. "They played a zone, and if you didn't attack it, they just sat there in the zone. We said we'll just hold it and see if they come out. It was as much his slow-down as mine. All they had to do is come out man for man, and they probably could have beat us."

The Terps held the ball for the last eight minutes of the game before it went into overtime. South Carolina led in overtime by five points before Maryland mastered arguably its most memorable finish in history. Jim O'Brien scored a layup. After a timeout, White stole the ball and Maryland scored again. After another timeout, Bob Bodell stole another Carolina pass, which led to O'Brien converting a nine-foot jump shot. Maryland held on to win, 31-30.

Driesell stood out among the throng on the court, the net cord draped around his neck.

McGuire told the *Baltimore Sun* afterward, "Something has gotten into this game that I don't like. It's not good for college ball. I don't know exactly how to describe it, but it's like a fever. It just doesn't seem normal."

Later that year, South Carolina, ranked sixth in the country, beat Maryland in the first round of the ACC tournament, 71-63. Lefty tried one more trick, switching his players' numbers at the tournament.

"It was sort of a joke to get our guys loose, just to screw those guys up, to say we can beat South Carolina," said Driesell. "I was telling our players those guys are so stupid they won't know who they're guarding."

The ploy created a problem Driesell had not anticipated. "It screwed up all the sports announcers and the radio people," he said. "I didn't do it to screw them up."

Midnight Mile

By the start of Lefty Driesell's third season as head coach, Maryland men's basketball had reached national prominence. They received a number six preseason ranking in the national polls, and for good reason. Sophomores McMillen, a preseason All-American, and Elmore joined such varsity veterans as White, O'Brien and Bodell.

Maryland got the season off to a conspicuous start by staging a one-mile timed run around the track in Byrd Stadium at 12:03 a.m. on October 15, the official NCAA practice starting date for men's basketball. Since Driesell became head coach at Maryland, the team started the season's first practice with the run. Those who didn't complete it in six minutes had to run it at the beginning of every practice until they did so.

Maryland was the first team in the country to start practice that season, and some considered it a publicity stunt.

"I did that to get the jump on people," said Driesell. "We were going to be the first ones to go to work and the last ones to play that season. And having the mile at the beginning of practice used to screw it up. The guys were too tired to practice."

About 400 people attended the run. Headlights from cars parked around the track provided light and helped prevent cheaters. Still, it wasn't enough to prevent some players from taking advantage of the situation.

"I heard later that Len Elmore cut some corners on me," said Driesell.

Elmore said with a chuckle that Lefty got it all wrong. "He kind of gets confused, it wasn't me," said Elmore, a freshman during the midnight run. "The guys cutting corners were juniors and seniors. If I cut corners and came in last, something was terribly wrong."

Elmore said finishing the run so poorly convinced him to improve his off-season conditioning. "I didn't feel good about coming in last," he said. "McMillen and I led the off-season and preseason practices. I made sure I did a six-minute mile. And I did a 10 minute mile and a half by the time I was a senior."

Lefty and Len Elmore

Tit for Tat with the Tar Heels

Maryland did not lose at Cole Field House that year. The biggest win came against North Carolina in mid-February, the second game between the two teams that season. McMillen called the first game between the two that year in Chapel Hill "not one of my greatest experiences."

The Tar Heels fans considered McMillan a traitor for choosing Maryland over North Carolina. Their jeering prompted head coach Dean Smith to plead for calm. One sign in the crowd read, "How's your mom, Tom," implying McMillen's mother had influenced his decision. North Carolina won that game by 20 points.

More than 15,000 people, the largest ACC crowd to date, packed Cole Field House for the February rematch. McMillen responded with 27 points and eight rebounds, helping Maryland clinch an invitation to the NIT tournament.

The Terps finished tied for second in the conference and advanced to the tournament final against none other than North Carolina, then ranked number three in the country. The Tar Heels won the final by nine points and finished third in the nation that year.

Maryland won the NIT by scoring more than 100 points and beating Niagara by 31. The team finished 27-5 and ranked 14th in the country. They set records for most victories, most points and most rebounds in a season. And McMillen and Elmore still had two years to go.

Helping Lay a Foundation

When Len Elmore took his recruiting visit to College Park, number of attractive coeds on campus. He said in the book *Maryland Basketball*, "When I came down on a recruiting visit, I said if the majority of the first 10 girls I see are good-looking, I'm coming here. About eight were good-looking."

Maryland fans liked what they saw in Elmore as well. The 6'9" center ended his Maryland career as the best rebounder in Maryland history with 1053. His season best of 412 in 1974 is almost 80 more than the next on the list, prompting Elmore to be named an All-American that season.

Elmore did not start playing basketball until he was in the 10th grade. He was a member of the National Honor Society at Power Memorial High School and used basketball to help deliver a message.

"The message was simple," said Elmore. "You don't have to be defined by the game. As an African American male, basketball was a means to a greater goal. You can use it in real life to reach back and help others. I wanted to be an example of someone who could use basketball as a means toward the ends of success after the game."

Elmore says he picked Maryland over St. John's and Princeton because Maryland did not have a long-standing tradition. "I wanted to lay a foundation so that years beyond, people would remember how it all got started."

Elmore left Maryland 18 credits short of receiving a degree. But he returned to Maryland for summer classes his first three years out of school and earned his degree while playing professional basketball. Elmore spent 10 years in the ABA and the NBA with five different teams. In 1987 he became the first former pro basketball player to graduate from Harvard Law School.

Getting to Know Ernie D.

With most of the team returning from the previous season, Maryland's 1972-73 squad received a number three national preseason ranking and was the favorite to win the ACC. It helped the Terps that the NCAA allowed two freshmen to play varsity, letting John Lucas and Mo Howard to join the top squad in their inaugural seasons.

Maryland lost by two points to NC State in the final of the ACC tournament, but advanced to the NCAA tournament because NC State was ineligible for NCAA postseason due to probation for recruiting violations.

Maryland lost to fourth-ranked Providence in the East Regional final, forcing Driesell to tears after the game.

Lefty also caused a few laughs during his interaction with Providence guard Ernie DeGregorio during the game.

"Lefty couldn't pronounce his name," said Lucas,. "So Ernie teased him about it. After every time he scored, he ran by the Maryland bench and said, 'Ernie DeGregorio.'"

There was reason for positive reflection at the season's end. Maryland finished eighth in the country. Senior Bob Bodell had not missed one game or practice during his career at Maryland. And Lucas served notice of his potential. He scored at least 20 points in each of the ACC tournament games, totaled 178 assists—the highest annual count of his Maryland career—and was selected to the All-Tournament team.

Living Up to the Hype

Expectations were understandably high of Tom McMillen when he entered the University of Maryland in 1971. He was a three-time high school All-American who averaged 47 points and 22 rebounds a game his senior year. McMillen said he was the victim of unreasonable expectations at Maryland.

He picked Maryland in part because he brother, Jay, played basketball in College Park and due to his father's preference of Driesell over North Carolina and Dean Smith. Joe Harrington, a friend of the McMillen family, said Mr. McMillen called Lefty "a man's man."

McMillen announced initially that he would attend North Carolina. The night before he was going to leave to attend Carolina, he changed his mind and picked Maryland, in part to be closer to his family.

"One of the reasons I picked Maryland was my father wasn't in the best of health," said McMillen. "Still, he drove down to every game, about five hours each way. And my father liked Lefty a lot."

After McMillen's father died while he was still at Maryland, Driesell surprised him by sending the entire team up to the funeral. "Those were the kinds of things Lefty did, said McMillen."

Further, President Nixon had appointed McMillen to the President's Council on Physical Fitness and Sports before he left high school. Attending Maryland made it easier for him to work on the council, which required occasional meetings at the White House.

Tom McMillen

"I was 18, here I am at a table with presidents of universities, with Roone Arledge, with Miss America," said McMillen. "I was just happy to be at the table."

In the book *Maryland Basketball*, McMillen called picking Maryland "a pioneering experience. If I chose North Carolina, I would have been perpetuating one."

McMillen, a premed-chemistry major, maintained a hectic schedule while in school. He served as the head of the Government's Commission on Student Affairs and led the effort to place the first student on the school's board of regents.

"I studied a lot," said McMillen. "There was not a lot of time for social diversions."

McMillen departed Maryland a three-time academic and athletic All-American and with career records for most points and best shooting percentage, among others.

He was also Maryland's first Rhodes Scholar. "The best thing about attending Maryland was the totality of the experience," he said. "It wasn't just playing basketball. It was most meaningful to me to win the Rhodes Scholarship. Maryland to this day has not had another Rhodes Scholar."

Still, his career ended with some frustration. McMillen said Maryland had goals of winning three national titles during his time in College Park. And the Terps lost in the ACC tournament finals three times while McMillen was on Maryland's varsity.

Almost the UCLA of the East

With a number four preseason ranking for the 1973-74 season, a national championship was not a far-fetched goal for the men's basketball team for the second consecutive season. Slimnastics exercises during practice, McMillen taking karate to increase his toughness and Elmore losing 20 pounds reflected the commitment in their preparation for the season.

Maryland opened up on the road against UCLA, which had won seven consecutive national championships and enjoyed a 76-game winning streak.

The key matchup in the game was centers Elmore and Bill Walton. Elmore almost didn't make the game. After his junior season, he considered entering the NBA rather than playing one more year for the Terps. He had endured a nagging knee injury that season and was unhappy with how he was scoring his points— mostly off of rebounds.

"I played with a lot of accomplished offensive players, such as Lucas and McMillen," said Elmore. "In some practices there wasn't a play for me for an hour. I would take a shot outside, and Coach said, 'Lenny, I don't want you shooting that shot.' I said, 'Okay, I won't shoot any more.'"

When Elmore told Driesell he was thinking about not coming back his senior year, he said Driesell told him he could do whatever he wanted, but just talk first to Red Auerbach.

"I stopped by his house," said Elmore. "He asked me how much am I going to make my first couple of years, one hundred, two hundred thousand? He said come back and have an All-American year, you'll be a much higher first-round pick. I expected to have an All-American year."

After Elmore decided to finish his senior season at Maryland, he and Driesell had a long talk. "He told me to get ready for the UCLA game, to prove that I was among the elite centers in America, to go out and show [Walton] what you're made of."

When he trained that summer on his own, Elmore told himself he would not let Walton embarrass him. He studied intensely, for a week, a tape of the previous year's NCAA title game in which UCLA beat Memphis State.

"I knew exactly what he was going to do," said Elmore. "I could read his hook. I threw Walton's first three shots into the second row. Walton said after the first one that it was goaltending. It wasn't. But the third one was."

Walton shot eight of 24 that game and scored 18 points. He also grabbed a peronal-best 27 rebounds. Elmore scored 19 points and grabbed 15 rebounds. Walton later called Elmore the best center he ever faced.

Maryland went on a 9-0 run late in the game to pull within one of the Bruins. They had the ball with about 10 seconds left, and worked a pick and roll with McMillen and Lucas.

"I lost the ball on the last play of the game," said Lucas. "The ball got tipped from behind, and as the ball was going out of bounds, Keith Wilkes saved it. As it was going out of bounds, he ran out and threw it downcourt. Mac and I had awful games."

John Lucas

Maryland's attempt to receive a number one ranking and officially become the UCLA of the east fell just short, 65-64. The loss forced sophomore Mo Howard, starting his first varsity game, to his knees at midcourt, weeping.

Maryland lost only three more games during the regular season, two to NC State and one to North Carolina. The Terps beat Duke by 21 and North Carolina by 20 in the ACC tournament, setting up another battle against number one-ranked North Carolina State, a team they had lost to five consecutive times.

In one sense, State was playing for a little more incentive in the final than was Maryland. They were banned from NCAA tournament play the previous year for recruiting violations. Only the ACC tournament champion qualified for the NCAA tournament. The loser had the choice of playing in the NIT, another postseason tournament.

Maryland shot 61 percent from the field in the classic battle. Howard hit two free throws to put Maryland ahead, 100-99. After David Thompson missed a field goal attempt, Lucas missed the first of a one-and-one free throw attempt. NC State then scored, and Maryland could not score during its last two possessions. The 103-100 loss is considered the most bitter in Maryland basketball history.

The postseason for Maryland, the fourth-ranked team in the country, amounted to another invitation to the National Invitational Tournament, which they won two years earlier. Maryland opted not to go.

Elmore blamed himself for the loss for allowing Tommy Burleson, State's 7'4" center, to score 38 points and grab 13 rebounds.

"In part because I followed our game plan, to make sure to point towards Thompson and not let him penetrate," said Elmore. "That allowed Burleson to set up deep in the paint. I allowed him to get good position because I was focused on Thompson. And people seem to forget I'm 6'9", Burleson's 7'4". He was no chump. He was a third-team All-American."

Some Maryland players and coaches felt it was unfair for Maryland to play the ACC tournament at Greensboro, North Carolina, located about an hour from Raleigh. Their appeals led to the ACC moving the tournament to the Capital Centre in Landover, Maryland, about 20 minutes from College Park, in 1976.

Lucas, McMillen and Elmore received All-American honors in 1974, the only time three Terps achieved that honor in one season. It was little consolation to the frustrating end to one of the more successful teams in men's basketball history.

Moses Passes by the Terps' Promised Land

With Elmore and McMillen graduated, Maryland was looking for a dominant big man for the 1974-75 season to complement guards Lucas and Howard, as well as sophomore Brad Davis and junior forwards Tom Roy and Owen Brown. Their best option was Moses Malone, a 6'11" introvert who led Petersburg (Virginia) High School to 50-0 record in his last two seasons.

While Malone was considering his college options, the Utah Stars of the American Basketball Association selected him in the 1974 draft.

Malone picked Maryland over Clemson and New Mexico. Malone's top choice seemed to be New Mexico, but he opted for College Park to be close to his mother, Mary.

Maryland's chances of playing in the NCAA tournament improved further in August, 1974, when the NCAA expanded the postseason tournament to 32 teams, including 12 at-large berths.

Then Malone deflated all the preseason hope and hype by signing with Utah and the ABA.

Lucas was Malone's roommate in College Park for one day. "We had a team meeting the day before he decided to go pro," said Lucas. "We offered him all our laundry money, which was about $1500 for the year. We thought that might make him stay for one year or two. He couldn't stop laughing when we did that."

Interestingly, Driesell referred Malone to sports agent Donald Dell to negotiate a fair contract with Utah. Malone reportedly signed for $2.65 million over seven years.

Lucas drove Malone to Dell's office in Washington and did not see him until two years later, when they were teammates with the Houston Rockets.

Malone wanted to feel a part of the Maryland team. He hung a Maryland uniform in his locker during the first year in Utah.

Better Fate Against State

With less expectation of a national title confronting them compared to the past few years, the men's basketball team flourished during the 1974-75 season. They finished the season ranked as they started, at number five, and won their first ACC regular season championship.

Driesell said after the season that the team accomplished more than any other he has coached.

A loss to third-ranked UCLA in the final of the Maryland Invitational Tournament during the winter holidays didn't dampen Maryland's spirits.

The first key conference matchup came against fourth-ranked NC State in mid-January. The dynamic David Thompson, who had averaged 31 points in six previous games against Maryland, was back for State, but not Tom Burleson. Thompson scored 33, but Lucas got 30 points and Maryland won for the first time in seven tries against State.

The next time the two teams played, Maryland had lost two in a row, to Clemson and North Carolina, and fell to eighth in the country. Thompson scored 38 in the game, but Brad Davis's short driving jumper with two second left won it for Maryland, 98-97. Maryland ended NC State's 37-game consecutive winning streak at home.

Cool Hand Luke

In a practice during the career of John Lucas, Lefty Driesell asked the clever guard to yell "gather" when he wanted him to set up a defensive formation. Lucas responded by saying the word in a mock falsetto voice.

Driesell expelled him from practice. "If he hadn't harped on me, I would have loafed," said Lucas in the book *Maryland Basketball*. "He did it so I wouldn't fizzle in games."

Lucas was much more dazzle than fizzle during his three years on the basketball team between 1974 and 1976. The interaction with Driesell that led to his dismissal from practice was typical Lucas—a moment of bold bravado peppered with a touch of charming showmanship. Lucas, in fact, was a lot like Driesell.

"He had great confidence, was outgoing, got along with people," said Driesell. "People just liked him. He was very confident. I loved John Lucas; he was a great leader for me. He was maybe the best leader I've ever had."

Lucas sees similarities between himself and his former coach. "Lefty has great compassion for people, and I think I have too," he said. "He's very quick-witted. Coach was very genuine to a fault. What you saw is what you got. And you don't have to wonder where you stand with me. I appear to have a lot gray areas, but he doesn't."

Len Elmore said both Lucas and Driesell were flamboyant. "Coach was humble in the newspapers, but we saw a very strong belief in himself," said Elmore. "That's terrific leadership. John was the same way. John came in as a freshman, and you think 'Where does this kid come off doing this?' You would laugh at him. He would wear turtlenecks and a leather coat and emulate John Shaft. He wanted to be Shaft, but he had never been to New York City. He was a populist kind of guy. That's the way Lefty was. And they were a both a bit manipulative. They knew how to direct people where to go.."

Elmore remembers when Lucas, who had been at Maryland a short time, drove around a traffic circle on campus in a Dodge Roadrunner for attention to "show how cool his car was," said

Lefty at Cole

Elmore, who was sitting in the car at the time. "Then a policeman stops us. He says, 'Mr. Elmore, will you tell this young man we don't do this on this campus?' It was an example of fresh exuberance."

Lucas, an All-American at Durham (North Carolina) Hillside High School, picked Maryland over more than 400 schools, in part because Driesell shook his hand in what Lucas called "a regular way. He didn't give me all that phony stuff," he said in the book *Maryland Basketball*. "That showed me he was honest."

Lucas ended his Maryland basketball days as a three-time All-American, the only basketball player to be so honored, and as the first Maryland player to earn first-team All-ACC honors for three successive seasons.

Lucas was also an All-American tennis player and a two-time ACC singles champion. "He had eyes like a hawk, and he moved very well, probably better than any tennis player that I had," said Doyle Royal, who coached Lucas on the Maryland tennis team. "He had a natural big left-handed serve, a nice forehand and a good volley. His backhand was suspect, but he was trying to improve it after basketball season."

Royal said Lucas could have been one of the best African American players in the United States. "At that time, the only black player who was real good was Arthur Ashe, who was getting ready to retire," he said. "I think he would have been the next top black player in the country. He was great to be around and the players liked him. He had a beautiful attitude."

A Season of Disappointment Laced with Tragedy

Maryland began the 1975-76 season with a number three preseason ranking and stayed true to the prognosticators by winning its first 11 games. Losses in three of its next five games, to number five-ranked North Carolina, number seven-ranked Wake Forest and unranked Clemson, contributed to the Terps ending up in second place in the ACC regular-season standings. The automatic NCAA tournament bid as regular-season champs went to North Carolina.

The ninth-ranked Terps needed a good performance in the ACC tournament to grab the at-large NCAA bid from the conference.

Despite the tournament being held at the Capital Centre near the Maryland campus, Maryland lost in the first round by eight points to unranked Virginia. The Cavaliers went on to win the tournament and claimed the NCAA at-large bid.

Maryland entered the ACC tournament with emotions strained beyond the pressures of college basketball. In early February, former Terp forward Owen Brown collapsed during a pickup basketball game at a Xerox training center in Northern Virginia and died. A stress test taken early in his Maryland career determined that Brown had an irregular heartbeat. Brown was aware of the danger, and examinations by a physician determined there was no abnormality and the risk for him to play basketball was acceptable.

"We had him checked and they said there was no blockage," said Driesell.

Driesell called Brown, who scored 1250 on his college boards, a brilliant person with a good spirit who liked to have a good time and who could have studied harder. His former players praised his determination and grace under pressure.

In April of that year, more tragedy struck the Maryland program. Chris Patton, who had just completed his sophomore year, died while playing a pickup game on the courts on the Byrd Stadium promenade across the street from the Ellicott Hall dormitory. It was determined that a ruptured aorta caused massive internal bleeding that led to Patton's death. Some experts claimed he suffered from Marphan's Syndrome, a genetic tissue disorder that can lead to heart attacks.

Patton was more withdrawn than Brown and was just blossoming in the Terp program before his death. He started the last four games of the previous season after suffering injures and illnesses during his first two years with the Terps.

On the heels of those two tragedies, the Maryland men's basketball team then endured two seasons of disappointment. Despite preseason rankings of eight and 14, respectively, Maryland failed again to qualify for the NCAA tournament and finished no higher than fourth in the ACC regular season. The glorious early years of the Driesell era suddenly seemed distant memories.

Kings of the Court

Albert King came to College Park as in 1977 as the nation's number one high school recruit. He averaged 38 points and 22 rebounds a game during his senior season. King blossomed his junior season in Maryland on a team that led the Terps back to ACC superiority.

King was named ACC Player of the Year and was the Terps' only All-American that season, and for good reason. He averaged 21.7 points a game, shooting more than 50 percent, and helped lead the Terps to their first ACC regular season title since 1974-75.

King also had ample support. Junior forward Ernest Graham, who holds the Maryland record for most points in a game (44 against N.C. State in 1978), was the Terps' leading scorer the previous season. Sophomore Buck Williams, a graceful center forward, led the ACC in rebounding the previous season and led the Terps on the boards as a sophomore.

A stretch in late January helped secure the Terps' success that season. Unranked Maryland followed a one-point win over Clemson with a six-point win over ninth-ranked North Carolina.

In the win over Clemson, Greg Manning lofted a six-foot jump shot over a Clemson defender after nearly falling down while running around an Albert King pick with five seconds remaining. The basket sent the first sellout crowd of the season in Cole Field house into a delirious state.

Ten days later, fifteenth-ranked Maryland traveled to South Bend, Indiana to play eighth-ranked Notre Dame. The Terps lost 64-63 after Notre Dame's Tracy Jackson drove the length of the court to score a layup with six seconds remaining.

Maryland rebounded four days later by beating thirteenth-ranked Virginia by two points in Charlottesville. Ernie Graham's 20-foot shot with five seconds remaining gave the Terps their first win against Virginia in six games.

The excitement continued through late February. Maryland had slowly risen to a number seven national ranking. And it entered the ACC tournament in Greensboro Coliseum as regular-season champions.

Maryland survived an overtime win over Georgia Tech in the first round and then beat Clemson by six points to advance to the tournament final.

On March 1, Duke derailed the Terps' momentum with a one-point victory. Albert King had made two foul shots to put the Terps up 72-71 with 55 seconds remaining, then Mike Gminski tipped in a Duke miss with eight seconds left to give the Blue Devils the lead. King then had a chance to win the game for Maryland

He shot over Gminski from the left of the key with time running out. The ball hit the front of the rim and around the hands of Buck Williams, who was trying to tap it in. Gene Banks grabbed the rebound and the unranked Blue Devils got the win they needed to advance to the NCAA tournament. Duke shot 79 percent from the field in the second half.

The loss reduced King to tears in the Maryland locker room following the game. King, who scored 27 points in the final and 38 in the first-round game, was voted the tournament MVP. He said the final was the most emotional game of his life.

Maryland beat Tennessee in the first round of the NCAA tournament and next faced local rival Georgetown. It marked the first time the two rivals played each other in the NCAA tournament, but not the first time they faced each other that season.

The Hoyas beat Maryland by 12 points in the Terps' third game of the season back in early December. The game had NCAA tournament intensity.

Toward the end of the first half, Georgetown coach John Thompson complained vehemently after a Georgetown player was given a technical foul for hanging on the rim following a dunk. Maryland forward Ernie Graham walked over to the enraged Thompson and patted the coach on the head.

"I was just telling him that he was too big to get that mad," said Graham in the *Washington Post*.

Thompson and Driesell then exchanged angry words in front of the scorer's table. One witness said Thompson swore at Driesell. After the game, Driesell refused to shake Thompson's hand. He also said Maryland would have "whipped their tails" if Buck Williams, out with a broken finger, had played the game.

Williams suited up for the NCAA clash, which was billed by the local media as the most significant game in the history of Washington-area college basketball.

Williams led the Terps with 18 points and 15 rebounds, but it was not enough to avoid a 74-68 defeat. Albert King scored only 15 points, well below his 21.7 points per game average. He didn't score in the game's last 18 minutes and fouled out with just more than one minute to play.

It was the end of a better-than-expected season for the Terps. But the excitement surrounding men's basketball in College Park would not be repeated for another four years.

Branch and Bias

Before Adrian Branch and Len Bias were teammates on the Maryland basketball team, they were friendly rivals from afar who lived close to each other. Both grew up within a 15-minute drive to College Park. Branch said he and Bias, one year behind Branch in school, never played against each other during that time. A friend often told Branch about how good Bias was, until he saw for himself one day.

"He was an extremely raw talent," said Branch. "He could jump over the moon. He had great strength and a soft touch." Branch played the game with more finesse than Bias. He was a pure shooter, and his floor style was smooth and sultry compared to Bias's more athletically dynamic style.

Both Branch and Bias were high school All-Americans and big-time programs pursued both players. Michigan, North Carolina, NC State and Maryland recruited Branch. When Dean Smith visited his house on a recruiting trip, Branch admits his ego was raging.

"Smith was sitting there talking to my parents, getting to know them, and I said to him, 'So when are you gonna give me a recruiting pitch?'" said Branch. "He said, 'Adrian, me knocking on your door means we want you to come to the university.' You never saw a big head shrink so quickly." Branch picked Maryland primarily because it was close to home. He had tired of all the traveling he had done with AAU teams since he was 12. "Why leave home when home's been so good to me?" said Branch, who entered Maryland with the hopes of becoming a train engineer. And with Albert King, Buck Williams, Ernest Graham and Greg Manning leaving the team, Branch figured he would see ample court time soon. He was right. His scoring average (15.2) and points for the season (442) as a freshman in 1981 rank second in school history behind Joe Smith.

That year, Branch hit the game winner against number one-ranked Virginia in the last regular-season game of the season. The 15-footer from the foul line fell through the basket as time expired. Branch scored 29 points, making 12 of 17 shots from the field. After the game, coach Lefty Driesell said Branch joined John Lucas as the best freshmen he ever coached.

Driesell overcame a minor mishap with Bias to land the All-Met player from Northwestern High School. Bias attended Driesell's summer camp the summer before his senior year of high school. Driesell was demonstrating how to use a fake and asked Bias to help him. When the coach asked Bias to jump when he faked a shot, Driesell's elbow hit Bias's lip. Bias, with his lip bleeding, ran off the court.

Bias possessed rare athletic skills. John Philbin was Maryland's assistant strength coach with the men's basketball team during Bias's freshman season. Philbin later was the U.S. Winter Olympic strength and conditioning coach and the head coach of the 1992 U.S. Olympic bobsled team. In the latter role, Philbin coached such noted athletes as Herschel Walker and Edwin Moses. Philbin rates Bias's athletic ability on the same level as Walker and Moses.

"He was one of the most talented athletes I've ever worked with," said Phlibin. "When you put a blueprint together to create the perfect basketball player, Michael Jordan comes to mind, and so does Bias. He was built like a thoroughbred horse. He was incredibly lean, had about five percent body fat. He could play either guard or forward. He had a vertical leap of 44 inches. He was a genetic freak, in a good sense. His ability to be explosive was unique."

Bias first started a game at Maryland in late February in his freshman year during the 1982-83, in the third to last game of the regular season against Wake Forest. From that point, Bias and Branch were two of the team's most reliable scorers through the 1984-85 season, when they were first (Bias) and second in scoring average.

It seemed destiny played a large part of the two developing close ties off the court as well. Branch was born on November seventeenth, Bias on November eighteenth, and both were six feet, eight inches tall.

"The first day Lenny got to Maryland, we went to Roy Rogers," said Branch. "I said, 'We're going to be here three years together, let's get along.' He said, 'Let's do it.' We were silly together, we were warriors together. There was an intimacy. When you go to war with somebody on the basketball court, there's camaraderie. Everybody loved Len. If Len let you into his world, he was a caring person with a tough exterior."

On some Sundays when they both attended Maryland, Branch stopped by the Bias house to pick up Len to go to campus and ended up staying for dinner. They would leave in Branch's Oldsmobile with 15 dollars for the week. By the time they reached campus, only five dollars remained after making a quick stop for some food.

During one of the visits to the Bias home, Branch learned that Bias's parents nicknamed Len "Frosty." "When he came home bundled up from the hospital after being born they said he looked like Frosty the Snowman," said Branch. "We'd go into their house, and his mom would say, 'How you doin' Frosty?'" said Branch. "I told my parents I wish we could be more like Lenny and his family. His brother, his sister, his mother and father would come up to his dorm and just visit with him. I think that was the greatest thing in the whole world."

Bias portrayed an engaging personality. Branch remembers Bias and teammate Jeff Baxter as the "best-dressed dudes in the ACC along with Johnny Dawkins. And Lenny was an incredible dancer. He loved [the television show] *Soul Train*. We used to love watching him dance."

Many loved the way both of them moved on the court as well. Bias was second on the team in scoring his sophomore season with a 15.2 average, one tenth of a point behind Ben Coleman and 1.8 points ahead of Branch. That year, Maryland won the ACC tournament for the first time since 1958.

The Terps won seven consecutive games on the way to winning the conference tournament. Branch had 18 points and Bias added 17 more in a win over Georgia Tech. Ben Coleman scored 26 points in a win over Wake Forest. Branch added 17, Bias 16. Branch led Maryland with 18 points in the next win over NC

State. He was the Terps' top scorer with 20 points in Maryland's next win over Virginia; Bias was right behind with 17 points.

Maryland earned its first ACC tournament win in three years with a first-round victory over NC State. Ben Coleman and Branch led the Terps with 16 points in a two-point semifinal win over Wake Forest. The game was not secure until Bias made a free throw with two seconds left.

Bias dominated the tournament final against Duke with a 26-point performance, hitting 12 of 17 shots from the field. The effort earned him honors as the outstanding player of the tournament. Bias said he entered the tournament with something to prove since he was not named to any All-ACC teams.

Maryland advanced to the Sweet 16 of the NCAA tournament, where they lost by two points to Illinois. Branch led Maryland in the game with 19 points. The Terps again advanced to the Sweet 16 the next season, but overall the season was not as rewarding for Maryland. They finished tied for fourth in the conference and out of the national rankings.

Still the Terps had some fine moments, compliments of Branch and Bias. Branch converted a 15-footer to send the season's first game against number two-ranked Duke into overtime, then made two free throws with eight seconds left in overtime to secure the win. Bias (24 points) and Branch (22) helped Maryland close a 14-point Duke lead in the second half.

With a 6-6 conference record, unranked Maryland was fighting for a favorable seed for the conference tournament with two regular-season conference clashes remaining. Jeff Baxter and Bias each made two foul shots in the final 12 seconds to secure a one-point win over NC State. Branch led Maryland with 23 points. He did the same in Maryland's next game, a five-point win over Virginia.

The Terps finished tied for fourth in the conference and lost to Duke in the first round of the tournament. Bias led Maryland in scoring that season with 19 points a game, .9 points ahead of the second-place Branch.

The bond between Branch and Bias was special. "He used to call me 'Cook,' because I'd be cookin' him on the basketball court," said Branch, who ended his Maryland career as a two-time all-ACC selection and later played in the NBA for five seasons. "There are a few dudes I'd go to war with. Lenny was one of them. I love Len. He was easy to love. He was a good dude."

On Top of the Basketball World

With Branch's eligibility expired, Bias handled most of the offensive battles for the Terps the next season. The Terps struggled early against ACC schools during Bias's senior year in 1985-86. They lost their first six conference contests.

Bias proved instrumental in helping the Terps recover. He scored a game-high 21 points in their first ACC win over Wake Forest and then 24 points in a nine-point win over Clemson. Against NC State in mid-February, he made the last two free throws of the game as the Terps won by one point for their third ACC win. Unfortunately for the Terps, Bias was in too much of a celebratory mood after the game. Bias and teammates Jeff Baxter and John Johnson were suspended for one game after missing a curfew following the win.

Coach Lefty Driesell noticed the players were missing after he heard a phone ring in one of the players' rooms while walking the halls of their hotel. When no one picked up the phone, Driesell entered the room and discovered the players missing. When they returned to the team hotel between 3 and 4 a.m. after visiting friends at the NC State campus, the coaches were waiting for them. Without the three players, Maryland lost to Clemson two days later.

Bias and his mates returned to the team in dramatic fashion for the Terps' next game against then number one-ranked and once-beaten North Carolina in the Dean Dome. With three minutes remaining and the Terps down by nine, Bias hit a 20-foot jumper and then performed a demonstrative slam dunk after he stole Carolina's inbound pass. One minute later, Bias blocked a layup by Carolina's Jeff Lebo and seconds later he hit a three-pointer to cut Carolina's lead to two.

In overtime, Bias converted the game-winning shot, a jump-hook through the lane, with just less than two minutes remaining. He then blocked Kenny Smith's soft hook shot, a potential game winner, to secure the victory for Maryland. Bias walked off the floor with 35 points in perhaps the most compelling performance of his Terp career.

Bias had a strong supporting cast in that melodrama. Baxter hit a 20-foot jumper with four seconds remaining to send the game into overtime. Keith Gatlin made two free throws to put Maryland up 75-72. Maryland got the ball back after North Carolina was called for a five-second violation trying to inbound the ball. On the next inbound play, Gatlin tossed the ball off Kenny Smith's back, caught the ball in bounds and made a layup that capped Maryland's 77-72 win.

Bias averaged 23 points in the Terps' last three ACC contests, in which they won two to finish 6-8, their worst showing in conference play in four years. On a bit of a roll, the Terps faced the Tar Heels in the first round of the ACC tournament. Bias scored 20 points in the game to become Maryland's all-time leading scorer. He also grabbed 13 rebounds as the unranked Terps beat fourth-ranked UNC by 12 points.

In the next game against Georgia Tech, Bias scored two of his game-leading 20 points with 12 seconds remaining to tie the game at 62. After Terry Long stole the ball from Mark Price, Maryland called time out with five seconds remaining. But Tech stole the inbound pass and scored the game winner on a dunk.

In his final game for Maryland, Bias scored 31 points, including the Terps' last 13 points, in an NCAA tournament second-round loss to UNLV, 70-64. Bias ended his career as one of the top players in college basketball. He was the ACC Player of the Year his junior and senior seasons, the only Terp basketball player to receive the honor twice. Those two years Bias led the conference in scoring and was an All-American as well.

The Boston Celtics solidified Bias's status by picking him second in the NBA draft later that year. But despite all the accomplishments, bring up the name Len Bias and most people will think of tragedy more than triumph.

"When I heard [Bias had died], I was incredibly numb, and anything else that goes along with it," said Branch, who works as a motivational speaker.

"He wasn't a monster or a bad guy. Sometimes people get themselves into something they can't get out of. How many people have done the same thing and lived? To this day, it's still one of the biggest mysteries in my life."

Maryland's Darkest Day

According to a report in the *Washington Post,* Bias initially celebrated the June 17 NBA draft in simple fashion. Bias stayed in Boston following the draft to meet with Reebok, his athletic apparel sponsor. He returned home with his father and sister Michelle on June 18. At around 11 p.m., he drove to his dorm at Maryland.

Keeta Covington, a defensive back with Maryland's football team, said he and basketball players Keith Gatlin, David Gregg and Jeff Baxter talked with Bias at the dorm about the Celtics' draft and Bias's future while they ate crabs until about 2 a.m.

Covington said Bias told him, "I'm getting away from here at about 2 or 2:15 a.m." He said Bias was not ill and that he was trying to get away from the phone. He said he was under the impression Bias was going to see a lady and was quoted as saying Bias returned to the dorm about 3 a.m.

Covington said Bias returned to campus about an hour after his departure after attending an off-campus party. According to grand jury testimony cited in court papers, Terry Long and David Gregg, Maryland basketball players who shared a dorm suite with Bias, said sometime after midnight Bias met a friend, Brian Tribble. The two went to Town Hall Liquors on Route 1 in College Park. At about 3 a.m., Bias and Tribble joined Long and Gregg back in the dorm. All four began snorting cocaine. According to the grand jury testimony, Tribble brought a coffee cup about halfway filled with cocaine into the room. The testimony said all four had used cocaine before.

Bias suffered three seizures after snorting the cocaine. At around 6:30, Tribble called 911. Bias was taken to Leland Memorial Hospital about two miles south of the Maryland campus. At the hospital, Dr. Edward Wilson, the chief emergency room physician, said Bias "was unconscious… he never spontaneously began breathing on his own. He had no organized heartbeat." Wilson said Bias was given five drugs in an attempt to revive him. After the drugs failed, Wilson said a pacemaker was implanted in the heart muscle to try to get it beating. That also failed, he said.

Bias was pronounced dead at Leland Memorial Hospital at 8:50 a.m. An autopsy report later revealed that Bias consumed three to five grams of cocaine before he collapsed and that the cocaine could have been contained in a beverage such as beer or soda. Maryland's chief medical examiner revealed that Bias died of "cocaine intoxication" after ingesting an unusually pure dose of the drug that stopped his heart within minutes.

Prince George's county prosecutor Arthur Marshall, who had convened a grand jury to investigate Bias's death, accused Lefty Driesell of obstructing the case. He said Driesell called the basketball players together at his house within two hours after Bias died and asked them not to talk to the police. It was later revealed that Driesell's financial advisor, Lee Fentress, told Driesell to clean up the room where Bias had snorted the cocaine with the others. Driesell relayed the order to Oliver Purnell, an assistant coach. The grand jury refused Marshall's request to indict Driesell.

As a result of the Bias death, university chancellor Dr. John Slaughter formed task forces to study academic performance and drug use at the university. Slaughter said he set up the academic task force because athletes expressed concerns about academics after Bias's death. "We were hearing that the athletes weren't receiving the kind of academic support that they needed, that they weren't being able to take the courses they wanted to take," he said. "Some of that was valid. It was clear that we needed to do more. And we wanted to establish more clear standards on our admissions policies. We set up admission standards that were stronger than all but Duke in the ACC.

"We set up the task force on drugs not because I thought the university was drug-ridden, but there were so many questions out there [about] whether or not it was a problem, or were they just accusations," said Slaughter. "And we needed to get the facts out. I knew the university was no worse than any other large university. And I think the facts indicated that."

Some four months after Bias died on October 29, Driesell resigned as coach to become an assistant athletic director at Maryland. He continued that role until he took the job as head coach at James Madison University 18 months later. Athletic director Dick Dull had resigned under pressure earlier in October. Football coach Bobby Ross resigned in late November.

When Bias died, the life of Maryland's athletic department changed in a way no one could have expected before the death.

Back Into Baltimore

Nearly 17 years after the death of Len Bias, current Maryland basketball coach Gary Williams said in the spring of 2003 that he still must recruit against others who reference the tragedy as a reason not to attend the school.

"It seems everybody we recruit gets press clippings of the Bias death sent to them by recruiters from other schools," said Williams.

Williams confronted another negative factor when he tried to recruit players out of Baltimore. The town known as Charm City was considered off limits to anyone associated with Maryland basketball for two reasons. Many in Baltimore felt Bob Wade, the beloved former coach of Dunbar High School, the city's beloved basketball team, was mistreated in College Park when he was fired after three seasons in 1989. And many also felt Baltimore native Earnest Graham, a Terp from 1978-1981, received a bad rap as a player with a bad attitude.

Following the worst season of his then 15-year college head coaching career and two successive losing seasons, Williams realized he had to tap into the Baltimore talent again for Maryland to be successful.

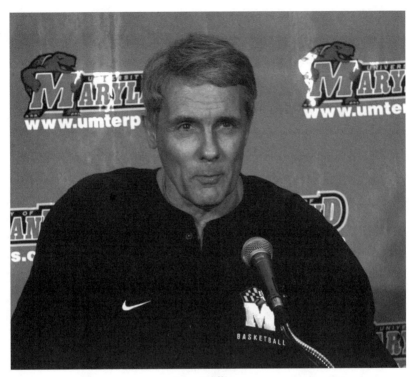

Gary Williams

His grassroots approach included attending Baltimore summer basketball league games, developing relationships with businessmen in the city and holding clinics there. The work paid off when Keith Booth, a high school All-American from Dunbar, picked Maryland over such teams as Kentucky and Duke in 1993.

"He was told by people from his community that he wouldn't get treated right," said Williams. Williams had relied on a handful of freshman recruits from the Washington, D.C. area—Dwayne Simpkins, Johnny Rhodes and Exree Hipp—to carry his team through the previous season. But now with Booth and an unheralded recruit named Joe Smith about to join the team in College Park, things were about to change for Maryland basketball.

Another Georgetown Classic

Joe Smith showed his value as a college basketball player in his first game. Unranked Maryland opened the 1993-94 season against 15th-ranked Georgetown at the old Capital Centre. The two teams had not played since Georgetown beat Maryland in the NCAA tournament in 1980.

The intimidating environment didn't matter to Smith. He scored 26 points and grabbed nine rebounds playing most of the game matched up against Othello Harrington, an All-American.

Gary Williams first saw Smith play the summer after his sophomore year in high school. "He was a skinny kid running all around the gym in a Norfolk Summer League game," said Williams. "He was kind of under the radar screen, but I saw that he loved the game. Sometimes kids have the talent, but they don't love the game. Joe always loved the game. I didn't know how good he was. But I knew he was good and better than I thought he was. When he came in the first day of practice, he was a dominating player. He could run well and jump well. The thing I didn't know was how well he shot. He had played on an AAU team with Allenn Iverson and didn't get to shoot that much."

Starting two freshman and three sophomores, Maryland fell behind in the second half of the Georgetown game, 51-37. They then stormed back after applying a full-court press and at one point led by four points late in the game. But Georgetown connected on a three-point basket with 4.6 seconds remaining, forcing overtime.

Maryland led by four in overtime after Smith made a basket and two free throws. But Georgetown scored seven straight points, including a desperation three-pointer from about 30 feet that banked in as the shot clock expired.

Booth made two free throws to pull Maryland within one with 39.2 seconds remaining. After reserve forward Kurtis Shultz stole a Georgetown pass, Maryland called timeout with 13.7 seconds on the clock.

Simpkins drove the lane and tossed in the game winner. "The last thing I told Duane was, 'If they're in the man-to-man, when you penetrate, make sure you drop it off to somebody for the shot,'" said Williams after the game in the *Washington Post*. "So he dropped it off in the basket."

After Georgetown failed to get a shot off on its last possession and the final buzzer sounded, Simpkins ran to the press table, slapped hands with Maryland radio announcer Johnny Holiday and jumped onto the table, arms raised in triumph.

Simpkins said after the game in the *Post* that he knew he was supposed to pass, not shoot. "Sometimes when I get in those situations, I want to be the hero," he said. Smith's heroics were evident. His 26 points were a school record for points scored in the first game of a player's career.

Williams called that win over Georgetown the most important game the Terps played until the national championship game against Indiana in 2002. The 1993-94 season began a string of 10 consecutive NCAA tournament appearances for the Terps and signaled the team's return to national prominence.

Goodbye Joe and Steve, Hello Juan

In early March 1995, the Terrapins were a team with renewed and consistent vigor, despite the temporary absence of their coach. They had shot up to number six in the country after Joe Smith tapped in the game winner at the buzzer in a 94-92 victory at Duke. Smith finished with 40 points, the second highest total against Duke since Len Bias scored 41 on January 26, 1986.

Williams missed the game due to pneumonia and did not return to the bench until Maryland played in the NCAA tournament almost two weeks later. In between, Maryland lost to North Carolina in the semifinals of the ACC tournament after sharing the ACC regular-season title. With a weakened Williams back on the bench, Maryland advanced to the Sweet 16, where they lost to eighth-ranked Connecticut.

Maryland also lost a big one the next day. Smith, the national Player of the Year in college basketball, had decided to turn pro. Smith left Maryland a two-time All-American and was one of only five players in Maryland history to average at least 10 rebounds and 10 points per game his entire career.

With junior Laron Profit leading the way, Maryland reached the Sweet Sixteen again in 1998. The next year, with one-year wonder Steve Francis leading the way, Maryland returned to the round of 16, but lost again.

Francis grew up in Silver Spring, Maryland, some five miles from the Maryland campus. Francis started only one game in high school, but came to Maryland as the top junior college prospect. Francis endured many struggles before becoming a Terp. He attended three different high schools while living with his grandmother after his mother died of a heart attack.

Francis led two different junior colleges to national titles. After their first 10 games that season, Maryland rose to a number two national ranking, in large part due to Francis.

Williams thought Francis would stay at Maryland for two years. But the scrappy guard decided to enter the NBA, leaving an opportunity for Francis's backup, the relatively unknown Juan Dixon from Baltimore, to sprout onto the scene.

Wonderful Juan

Gary Williams first saw Juan Dixon play in an AAU Summer League game in Georgia on a hot summer day in 1996. Dixon's team was losing by 20 points with about two minutes remaining. But one guy was diving for loose balls, trying to win the game. It was Dixon.

Dixon had been a scrapper all his life. He was forced to live with his maternal grandparents after his parents spent much of his young life in jail for drug abuse. By December 1995, Dixon's last year of high school, both of his parents had died from complications of AIDS as a result of drug use.

The following summer, Williams saw Dixon's frenetic style of play for the first time. And he liked what he saw. Dixon picked

Maryland over George Washington University, Providence College and Xavier University of Louisiana. After his sophomore season, he showed that Williams had pulled off a recruiting coup.

Dixon was the leading scorer on a team that finished second in the ACC regular season and lost to Duke in the ACC tournament championship game. The next year, Dixon again was the leading scorer on a team that advanced to the NCAA Final Four for the first time in history.

In that NCAA semifinal, the number 11-ranked Terps faced number one-ranked Duke. Maryland endured two heartbreaking losses to Duke in the regular season. In the first game, Maryland lost the game in overtime after leading by 10 points with one minute remaining. Maryland senior Mike Mardesich called it the worst loss of his career.

Maryland then lost four of its next five games, including one to conference lightweight Florida State on Valentine's Day. The poor Terps effort yielded a flurry of boos from the home crowd. Williams wondered if Maryland would win another game that season.

Despite his anxiety, Williams was unusually calm the next day at practice. "At our lowest moment, he had a cool head," said Mardesich in the book *Sweet Redemption*. "That turned our season around."

Maryland then won its next seven games, including an 11-point victory over number two-ranked Duke in Durham. The Terps tried to make it eight in a row against Duke in the ACC tournament semifinals, but lost by two points on a tip-in by Duke with 1.3 seconds left in the game.

The drama between the two continued in the NCAA clash. Aided by many of Juan Dixon's 16 first-half points, Maryland shot out to a 39-17 lead after 13 minutes. But Duke fought back to within 11 points at halftime and its first lead with six minutes and 50 seconds to play. A Terrence Morris free throw with five minutes to play gave Maryland its last lead. Miraculously, the Terps lost that game by 11 points. The loss did not demoralize the Terps. Instead, it created a sense of resolve that resulted in a

Cole Field House

prompt return to getting ready for the next season, lifting weights and playing basketball again.

Final Four? Not Good Enough

Gary Williams put his team on the spot at the last Midnight Madness in Cole Field House on October 13, 2001. He told a packed arena that Maryland wanted to win the national championship.

Williams's prediction was not that far-fetched. Maryland lost just one senior starter, Terrence Morris, from the Final Four team of the previous season, and two other seniors. Seven of the Terps' eight top scorers returned.

The number three-ranked Terps had lost twice when they met Duke for the first time that season in mid-January. The number one-ranked Blue Devils won by 21 points. But this time the Terps did not collapse after a Duke loss. They won their next 13 games on the way to a 15-1 ACC regular-season finish, the best in team history, and the regular-season championship. The Terps capped the regular season with a demonstrative 20-point victory over Virginia in the last game played at Cole Field House, scoring 112 points. They put on a good show in front of such former Maryland basketball greats as Len Elmore, Buck Williams, Tom McMillen and Keith Booth, who all attended a special ceremony.

A loss to NC State in an ACC semifinal by four points did not put a dent in the Terps' destiny. A number one seed in the east regional of the NCAA tournament certainly aided the Terps' cause. Ranked number four in the country, Maryland cruised past its first two opponents in the NCAA tournament, Sienna and Wisconsin. In the win against Wisconsin, Dixon became Maryland's all-time leading scorer after he tallied 29 points.

Against Kentucky in the round of 16, Maryland used their advantage inside with bruiser Lonny Baxter and cruiser Chris Wilcox to beat Kentucky by 10 points. Against Connecticut in the round of eight, the strong inside play of Baxter kept Maryland in the game, while the determination of Dixon carried the Terps to victory. With Maryland down by three with five minutes remaining, Williams called timeout and Dixon took over. "Give me the ball, and I'll take you to Atlanta," he said to Williams, as reported in the book *Sweet Redemption*.

Dixon converted a three-pointer on Maryland's next possession. Steve Blake made his first points of the game, a three-pointer with 25.4 seconds left, to give Maryland a six-point lead. Maryland won by eight, and was on the road to its second consecutive Final Four.

Chris Wilcox showed Kansas what they were in for in their semifinal game against Maryland when he blocked All-American Drew Gooden's first two shots. After falling behind early, Maryland battled back for a seven-point halftime lead.

Dixon played a large part in the Terps' recovery late in the half. Maryland trailed by two with about eight minutes remaining in the first half. Maryland came out of a timeout in a trapping zone defense, and after Kansas missed a shot, Dixon grabbed the rebound, brought the ball down court and converted a three-pointer from the right side, giving Maryland its first lead of the game, 26-25.

Seconds later, Maryland scored again after Dixon stole the ball from Nick Collison while the Kansas forward dribbled near the foul line. Later, Dixon duped Kansas guard Jeff Boschee into fouling him during a three-point shot. Dixon had a clear look for the three-pointer until Boschee jumped aggressively toward him and altered his shot to draw the foul.

Dixon had scored 19 points with a couple minutes remaining in the half. Maryland stretched its lead to 20 with about six minutes remaining. But sloppy play by the Terps ensued, and Kansas fought back to within five points with just more than two minutes remaining.

Dixon again took charge for the Terps when they needed it most. After a Kansas turnover, he hit a three-pointer from the baseline, and Maryland cemented the win with proficient free throw shooting. Maryland showed little elation after that win. There was one more game to go to live up to the promise that coach Williams had made back on October 13.

Williams said Indiana, the Terps' opponent in the final, was the first surprise team they played in the tournament. The Hoosiers had upset Duke and Oklahoma. There was an unsettling sense in the locker room before the game. An emotional Juan Dixon, crying at times, asked his teammates to help him win the game.

Dixon scored 11 points in the first 10 minutes, but neither team played well in the first half, which ended with Maryland leading by six points. After Indiana went up by one point with about eight minutes remaining for its first lead in the game, Dixon came back to hit a three-pointer. Maryland then went on a roll, holding Indiana to three points from the seven-minute mark until the final seconds.

A play by Byron Mouton secured Maryland's win. He chased down a Blake miss and while falling out of bounds threw the ball back out to Blake, maintaining Maryland's possession. The play led to a Steve Nicholas basket.

When Mouton transferred to Maryland, he told Williams he was doing so to win a national championship. The 64-52 win over Indiana helped Mouton fulfill his prophecy.

A scene at the end of the game typified the father-son type of relationship that had blossomed between Williams and Dixon. With the Terps' 12-point lead and the game's final seconds fading, Indiana was letting Maryland comfortably possess the ball to allow Maryland to savor the final moments. While embracing the scene, Juan Dixon was called for a five-second violation on Maryland's offensive end for not advancing the ball to the basket. With the game in hand and his players celebrating behind him on the bench, Williams shouted to Dixon, wanting to know why he committed the turnover.

Dixon again possessed the ball when the game ended, and this time there was no violation. Instead, he tossed the ball skyward in jubilation. Later, Williams approached Dixon and showed him that all was forgiven.

A Well-Respected Program

Chris Weller remembers vividly the first time Maryland's women's basketball team played a game on national television in 1974. Not only because the Terps lost by 32 points to defending national champion Immaculatta, but also because Weller's mother made such a big deal about her daughter's conspicuous appearance.

During the game in January that year, Weller, an assistant coach under Dottie McKnight, wore a green suit. After the game, Weller's mother focused on how good she looked in the suit. "But I was so pissed that we lost," said Weller. "I said, Mom, we lost by 32 points."

Maryland teams with Weller as coach rarely suffered such defeats. And they were part of a few moments that were firsts for women's athletics.

The game against Immaculatta was the first national television broadcast of any women's college basketball game.

When Weller took over as head coach of the team in 1975, Dottie McKnight had made the program one of the best in the East, with a 44-17 record in four years.

Weller quickly transformed the team into a nationally recognized program. Weller's team appeared in the championship game of the first AIAW National tournament in 1978, losing to UCLA. That year, Maryland was also the first ACC women's basketball tournament champion. They would win seven more titles, including five of the first six contended. In 1982, the Lady Terps appeared in the first NCAA women's Final Four, losing to Cheyney State in a semifinal game. Weller was women's basketball head coach a remarkable 27 years, the longest tenure of any women's coach at Maryland.

Weller's Maryland athletic career began in 1962, when she first played on the women's basketball team she said was called an "interest group." They practiced and played their home games at Prinkert Field House, which allowed for a standing-room crowd of only 25 people.

"We had a real home-court advantage," said Weller. "We knew where the bad spots were. At one end, you would slide into the wall. At the other end, there were splinters in the floor. And there was no concept of training."

Still, Maryland managed an undefeated record when they traveled to Immaculatta College later in her playing career. "We figured they wouldn't be any challenge, so we stopped at McDonald's for a meal before the game," she said.

Maryland lost the game. "We felt horrible," said Weller. "So we offered to take Coach McKnight out to dinner, at a Hot Shoppes in Langley Park. But she knew we felt horrible, and she treated us."

Weller also was a member of the women's lacrosse and swimming "interest groups" at Maryland.

"We took care of the field ourselves," said Weller. "If it had holes, we'd bring dirt and plant some seeds and water it. It sounds a little bizarre. What was wrong with us? We were college kids. We got a coach ourselves and ran the schedule ourselves. It was fun. I just liked to compete."

Weller transferred that competitiveness when she became an assistant coach for McKnight for the 1973-74 season for a $300 graduate assistant stipend. Weller accepted Kehoe's offer to be the head coach the next season at the age of 30. "My father was upset with me because he thought I was committing financial suicide," said Weller.

Weller says Kehoe made her take the job as first women's athletic director in Maryland's department of intercollegiate athletics, a position she held until 1980. "I told him my goal was to have all the women's coaches reporting to the same athletic director as the men's coaches," she said. "I wanted the student athletes to have the same kind of programs and opportunities as the men.

Weller battled at times with Kehoe, but she said that while he was tough, he was also fair. During her third year as coach, Weller noticed she was $800 short in her budget following the AIAW Final Four loss to UCLA. Weller was afraid to tell Kehoe, so she planned to pay for the loss out of her salary. The total amounted to two of her paychecks.

Before she could pay the money back, Kehoe called her into his office. "He said I hadn't reconciled the Final Four budget yet," she said. "I was crying, telling him I was taking the money out of my paycheck. He says, 'Well, that's a rough way to learn a lesson.'"

Kehoe later found out that the women's team was billed an $150 entry fee to play in the tournament. "He said, 'That is the most ridiculous thing I have ever heard,'" said Weller. "I just spent 10-15 thousand dollars sending my team to a national tournament, and now they want me to pay an entry fee? You're costing me money to win.' I said, 'I know, Mr. Kehoe, but one day that will not be the case.' When I would ask him for things, he would fuss about it. But he would often walk back into my office and say, 'How much?'"

A Little Help from Lefty

Weller says she and men's coach Lefty Driesell worked well together as they were both developing their programs.

Early in her career, Weller didn't have enough quality players for a practice squad, so she recruited male students to practice against her girls' team. During one practice a week before a game against Old Dominion, then one of the top programs in the country, the male students failed to appear.

"Lefty came over and said, 'What do you need, Coach?' I said 'They're huge. There is a big left-hander who shoots hook shots, and she's always setting up on the right block.' Lefty said, 'Okay, we can get a group here.' He gets his managers and they were running full-court with my team. Myra Walters, our five-foot-10 center, is guarding him. Lefty is running up and down the court, posting up on the right block. I'd say, 'Get in front of him, get in front of him.' I wish I had filmed it. Everybody thinks of Lefty and don't respect him enough. He's a wonderful man."

That does not mean the two coaches didn't clash at times. Weller says Lefty tried to persuade her to practice in Ritchie Coliseum. "He said you can really develop an atmosphere there," she said.

Weller wanted to practice where she played the games, in Cole Field House. "They told us there were no locker rooms available," she said. "They said there was no court time. I said 'We'll practice after the men.' Then he said, 'You know, a lot of people like to practice early in the morning, then you've got your whole day. I said, 'No, we'll practice right after you.' We'd always hope they'd have a good practice, so we could get started on time.

"Sometimes, after a bad practice, we'd start at 7:30. Lefty was a good competitor, but he treated us with respect that one competitor shows another."

Weller's Wonder Years

From the 1977-78 to the 1982-83 seasons, the women's basketball team at Maryland was ranked from sixth to eighth in the country.

The 1977-78 season was one of the best in Lady Terps history. They were the first ACC champions, and they finished the season ranked sixth in the nation after losing to UCLA in the AIAW championship game, indicative of the women's national collegiate championship. The game was played in front of 9,351 fans, the largest to watch a women's title game.

Scrappy senior guard Tara Heiss, named to the U.S. Olympic team in 1980, that season set the school record for assists in a game with 17 against Rutgers.

The Lady Terps won the ACC title the next five seasons and reached the AIAW quarterfinals three more times during that stretch.

The NCAA took over the women's national collegiate championships in 1981-82, and Maryland made an immediate impact. The Lady Terps hosted the first women's NCAA tournament game at Cole Field House in the first round and beat Stanford by more than 30 points. Maryland advanced to the Final Four, where they lost to Cheyney State, and finished the season ranked third in the nation, the highest in the history of the program.

After Weller won her 150th game as Maryland's coach that year, her players presented her with a bouquet of flowers in a hotel room. "I didn't care about the 150th win," said Weller in the *Washington Post*. "What did mean a lot was the flowers."

For good reason. That kind of appreciative act bestowed upon Weller would have been an unlikely gesture a few years prior. Four members of Maryland's team that lost in the national final to UCLA transferred. Center Kris Kirchner, the team's leading scorer and rebounder in 1980, transferred after that season, after publicly stating her dissatisfaction with Weller.

Weller admits Kirchner's departure "hurt a lot." She admitted in the *Washington Post* that she was doing too much as the school's basketball coach and women's athletic director, which she quit in 1980. "I really didn't know enough about my team," she said in the *Post*.

"I was not as careful about individuals as I should have been."

Weller showed her new approach after the team won the west regional in 1982. Weller had scheduled a practice the day the team returned from the trip, but changed her mind after the players talked her out of it."

An Ebb and Flow Period

The Lady Terps had the best start of any Weller team in the 1982-83 season. Led by senior All-Americans Debbie Lytle, a guard, and Yugoslavian Jasmina Perazic, a guard/forward, they won their first 16 games, still a school record for consecutive games won, and had reached a number three national ranking before losing to NC State in Cole Field House by five points.

Maryland later beat seventh-ranked Old Dominion by 16 points. By the time they entered the ACC tournament, the Lady Terps were 22-4 and ranked seventh in the country. They avenged two losses to NC State by beating the Wolfpack by three points in the tournament final.

Old Dominion served some vengeance of their own on Maryland, beating them by 17 points in the NCAA tournament's round of 16.

Perazic led the team in scoring her junior and senior years, while Lytle was the team's assists leader all four years she played varsity.

The women's basketball team relinquished its dominance on the ACC a bit from 1983 to 1987, winning the conference tournament title just once during that time. In 1985, Maryland ended its first season with a losing record. Weller admits she was distracted that season when her mother suffered a stroke.

The next season, Maryland finished the regular season 14-12, but won each game in the ACC tournament by at least 15 points on the way to the tournament title. The 1987-88 and 1988-89 teams were two of Weller's finest. In 1987-88, the Lady Terps did not lose at home. Forward Vicky Bullett set all-time scoring and rebounding records as a junior and won a gold medal with the U.S. team at the Summer Olympics later that year.

Many consider the next season the best in Maryland women's basketball history. They again were undefeated at home, and finished with a 29-3 record. It was the most wins in a season for the team. Their only conference loss was to Clemson, by two points. The closest conference game Maryland endured was five point overtime win against Virginia in Charlottesville. Sophomore Takisha Ward made two free throws with one second remaining in regulation to send the game into overtime. Tate scored 24 points and added 11 assists in the game.

After the game, Weller said the Lady Terps needed such a game because they were winning tough games by large margins. The Lady Terps won a school record 21 consecutive games, including victories in the first two rounds of the NCAA tournament at home. Maryland's backcourt stole the show for Maryland in the Terps' next game, an eight-point win over Texas on the Longhorns' home court. The win sent the Lady Terps to the NCAA Final Four for the second and last time in Maryland history. In the game, senior Deanna Tate scored 32 points, a career high, and backcourt mate Carla Holmes, a sophomore, added 28.

Perkins Provides Some Perks

Weller relishes the effort made by athletic director Lew Perkins in support of her team during the NCAA tournament run. Perkins allowed the school pep band to attend the game against Texas. Perkins flew parents of all Maryland's coaches to the Final Four in Tacoma, Washington. He also treated the team to what Weller calls a "fancy restaurant. We were used to eating at Denny's and Shoney's," she said.

Despite the first-class treatment, Maryland's winning streak ended with a 12-point loss in the Final Four to Tennessee. Bullett was voted ACC Player of the Year, and she and guard Tate earned Kodak All-America honors. Weller also received an unexpected gift. When she returned from the Final Four, she discovered a bonus of a month's salary for her and her coaching staff.

The 1988-89 team provided Weller with some of the more fond memories of her career. During the last road trip of the regular season, the players staged a talent show in the hotel where they stayed. "They were imitating singers," said Weller. "But I didn't get it. I didn't know who they were. I would say, 'Who's that?' Bullett won hands down for her Stevie Wonder imitation. Subrena Rivers, Christy Winters, Tate and Kiaisa Maine imitated a rap group."

Weller claims those kinds of moments symbolized the special level of camaraderie of that team. Bullett placed inspirational thoughts on her teammates' lockers.

During the next 13 seasons, Weller's teams never matched the magic of that 1988-89 team. One season that came close was the 1991-92 season, when Maryland reached the Elite Eight of the NCAA tournament for the last time. Also that season, Maryland earned its first-ever number one national ranking.

It came after third-ranked Maryland beat top-ranked Virginia by two points in Charlottesville after almost losing a 14-point lead. Maryland held onto the number one-ranking for four weeks and boasted an 11-game win streak when it hosted number two-ranked Virginia on February 11.

It was one of the most classic regular-season games in the history of women's collegiate basketball. The first sellout crowd for a women's game at Cole Field house greeted the two teams. The 14,500 official fans at the game outnumbered the previous best crowd by four times. But two rows of standing-room-only spectators circled the arena's concourse. The *Diamondback* reported it was more than the combined home attendance total from the previous season.

The game was close throughout, with Virginia leading at halftime by two points. The Cavaliers held on to win, 75-74.

Weller retired from Maryland following the 2002 season with 499 wins and 286 losses. She says when she graduated from Maryland, her major goal was to feel like she never worked a day in her life and to never be a prisoner of her possessions. "That way you can be more passionate about it," she said.

Chris Weller's passion for women's basketball at Maryland was on prominent display throughout the 27 years she served as the team's head coach.

22

Claiborne a Good Call

Maryland considered Jerry Claiborne for the football head coach's position in 1958 and 1966, but it was not until 1972 that Claiborne and the school agreed that they were right for each other.

Claiborne entered Maryland as a well-traveled coach. He was an assistant to Bear Bryant at the University of Kentucky, Texas A&M, and Alabama. He served under Frank Broyles at Missouri and worked as an assistant to Eddie Crowder at Colorado in 1971, when the Buffaloes finished third in the nation.

Claiborne was also head coach at Virginia Tech for 10 years, leaving the school with a 61-37-2 record and two trips to the Liberty Bowl. He was fired from Tech, he says, because he was honest about the recruiting situation at the school.

Kehoe thought Claiborne would eventually become the head coach at Colorado. "But he called me," said Kehoe. "If he hadn't called me, we probably would have never considered him."

A stark contrast to Lefty Driesell's charisma and charm, Claiborne radiated a cloaked intensity. His no-nonsense approach at times seemed cold and calculated. A religious man who did not drink or, for the most part, swear, Claiborne emanated a holy aura. And he did as he said. "He practiced what he preached," said 1974 graduate Paul Vellano, an All-American defensive tackle, in the book *Maryland Football*. "He wanted us neat, and he was always neat. He taught us concentration and dedication. He gave us leadership."

Bryant remembers one time when Claiborne did let a profanity leak. Claiborne was a good student at Kentucky. When Claiborne took a tennis class, he expected to get an A. He instead received a disappointing C. "It's the only time I've ever heard him swear," said Bryant in the book *Maryland Football*.

Ralph Larry, the first Terp football player to earn four All-ACC academic honors, remembers Claiborne as a respected teacher more than an affable mentor.

"He was somebody you respected and you learned life lessons from, as opposed to somebody you love being with," he said. "I can't remember a single time I was comfortable around him. I always felt like I had to be on my toes. You had to watch what you said. He made me want to make him happy.

"He was a straightforward guy. When he got pissed off at you, he got pissed off because you did something stupid. When you did something well, or when you did something bad, he'd let you know."

Larry's experience when Claiborne recruited him says a lot about the coach. Larry, an All-Met selection out of Rockville, Maryland, initially had interest from Maryland, Boston College and William & Mary. Each one, in succession, ultimately said they would not be offering a scholarship.

Larry's disappointment convinced him to consider taking a college baseball scholarship. Then Maryland assistant Joe Krivak called Larry and said if he was still interested in a scholarship at Maryland, to stop by the football office immediately and talk about it.

"So my dad and I got in our Pinto from Rockville and got there in the afternoon," said Larry. "He said somebody from North Carolina had backed out of a scholarship and that Krivak recommended me to Claiborne because he said I was smart. He said, 'You're not very strong, and you're not very fast. And I'm not sure if you'll ever play here at the University of Maryland. But if you do come here, you'll help us with the team grade point average.' I don't know if he really believed that was the case or if he was throwing the gauntlet down. My dad and I look at each other and said, 'Who cares?' We figured it was a way to get in the door."

Larry, nicknamed Buffalo Head because he "loved to knock the snot out of people," graduated from Maryland with a 3.3 grade point average. And he started at safety for Maryland for three seasons.

Forgetting the Immediate Past

Claiborne wanted to change the way his players approached the game. "These players have been kicked around and criticized long enough," he said in the book *Maryland Football*.

"What they really needed was a positive approach. We didn't want to look back. I didn't care what had happened before I arrived. I wanted to look forward."

Claiborne turned Maryland's football program around immediately. Maryland led the ACC in defense in his first season, one year after finishing last in the conference. Twelve starters returned to the 1973 team, and Claiborne used the talent to produce an 8-4 season, Maryland's first winning record since 1962. The Terps finished second in the ACC and played in a bowl game for the first time in 18 years. They lost to Georgia by one point in the Peach Bowl.

Vellano had a lot to do with the Terps' success. The defender often kept his teammates loose with his fun-loving personality. He had a tattoo of a Terrapin placed on his upper leg to "really identify with the school," he said in the book *Maryland Football*.

By the 1974 season, a lot more people were identifying with the Maryland football program. With a number 11 preseason ranking, their first national ranking since 1961, the Terps opened up the season at home in front of a record crowd of 54,412 in Byrd Stadium with a five-point loss against former Terp coach

Bear Bryant and number three-ranked Alabama. The Terps lost to unranked Florida the next week.

They then won eight of their next nine games, losing only to 10th-ranked Penn State by a touchdown. A loss to Tennessee in the Liberty Bowl gave the Terps another 8-4 record.

Bryant said he initially scheduled Alabama's game against Maryland so his players could enjoy some sightseeing in Washington. "Now, the only sightseeing they will do is on the bus from the airport to the hotel," he said in the book *Maryland Football*. Despite the win, Bryant said Maryland beat Alabama physically.

After the Florida loss, Claiborne replaced injured quarterback Ben Kinard with Bob Avellini. The offense scored 24 points against a North Carolina team that had not given up a point in eight quarters. Louis Carter ran for 158 yards, including a 76-yard jaunt around the right end in the second quarter, a play Claiborne said he had been looking for all season.

It was Maryland's first of five successive wins, the last being a 20-10 win over NC State. While watching films from the game between the two teams the previous season, the Terps noticed Wolfpack players taunting kicker Steve Mike-Mayer after he missed a last-minute field goal attempt.

"If you have any kind of pride, you don't want that stuff happening again," said Maryland All-American defensive tackle Randy White in the book *Maryland Football*. "We were more emotional about this game than any this season."

Carter ran 180 yards that day, the best one-game performance of his career. Mike-Mayer converted two field goals. The win put the Terps atop the ACC standing at 4-0. Wins later against Duke and Virginia clinched Maryland's first ACC title since 1955.

In the 24-17 loss to Penn State, Maryland outgained the Nittany Lions 407-298. On fourth down and time running out, Avellini admitted he threw over the head of Alan Bloomindgale, who had an open run to the end zone. Still, Avellini threw for 302 yards that day, the second best performance of his career.

White was ACC Player of the Year, the first Terp to be so named since Bob Pellegirini in 1955. He also received the Outland Trophy as college football's best interior lineman and the Lombardi Trophy, given by the coaches' association to the best lineman in college football.

"At that point of my career, I was just enjoying playing football," said White. "I really didn't realize what it meant to win those awards. I was just scared to death trying to help Maryland football win football games. I was always of the opinion somebody was going to take my job. I never worried about the honors."

White Is Right

Roy Lester struggled as Maryland's football coach, leaving after three years with a 7-25 record. But he left an indelible legacy in College Park with his ability to recruit a fullback and linebacker out of Thomas McKean High School in Wilmington, Delaware named Randy White.

White was recruited by Maryland, Arizona State and Virginia Tech. The early efforts of Lester's chief recruiter, Dim Montero, who first contacted White as a sophomore, helped convince White to attend Maryland. White was also an All-State basketball player and batted over .500 his senior year of high school.

When White visited Maryland, Lester told him he didn't know if White was good enough to play at Maryland, but he was going to give White a chance to show what he could do.

"It made no difference to me," said White. "All I knew is I got a four-year scholarship. I just wanted to make the team."

White played fullback his freshman year. During a meeting the following spring, Claiborne changed the path of White's football career. He asked White if he wanted to be an All-American and if he knew what it took to be an All-American. Claiborne said it took dedication. "I told him he could make himself into whatever he wanted," said Claiborne in the book *Maryland Football.*

Randy White and Jerry Claiborne

The meeting was brief," said White. "Claiborne was a man of few words. He always carried a presence where he was intimidating. He was tough, hard, and told you what he expects of you."

One thing Claiborne told White to do was lift weights, something White had never done before. When he started weight conditioning, he could bench-press only 210 pounds.

"All the others are benching 300 pounds," he said. "I didn't feel comfortable being around those guys, so I used to sneak in the weight room early and late, when no one else was there. I didn't want anyone to see me lift weights."

White worked up to the strength level of his teammates after about eight weeks of mostly solitary workouts up to six days a week, in a small, sweaty, dungy, hot gym in the back of Cole Field House, near the tunnel that led the basketball players to the floor. White said a significant moment in the Maryland football program took place in the gym during an off-season workout before the 1973 season.

"We're making some noise, and Lefty's team is practicing," he said. "He sends somebody back to tell us we're making too much noise, that we're interrupting his practice. We're interrupting their practice? We then made so much noise from that point, it was kind of like we're going to make this team better than yours. That was a turning point for us."

White transformed himself into one of the best defensive tackles to ever play college football. At the time of the talk with Claiborne, White weighed 223 pounds and ran the 40-yard dash in 4.9 seconds. By the end of his senior year, he gained 25 pounds, ran the 40 in 4.6 and bench-pressed 450 pounds. With the new strength and increased speed, Maryland coaches transformed White into a dominating stand-up defensive end in the wide-tackle six formation.

During the 1973 season, White enjoyed what he said was his most memorable moment at a Terp football player. After a season-opening loss to West Virginia, Maryland faced North Carolina in Chapel Hill in the second game of the season, against a team that had the longest winning streak in the country.

"We were a bunch of kids who had never been nowhere," said White. "All those people with blue on. When you went to North Carolina, you didn't know what to expect. We whipped them in the back yard [23-3]."

As aggressive as White was in his training and playing, he was humble and quiet off the field. His teammates pushed him forward during one press conference. After the Cowboys made him the second pick in the 1975 draft—the highest ever for a Maryland football player—they talked of turning him into a linebacker.

White said he didn't care where he played, he just wanted to play football. Maryland fans are surely grateful he played his college football in College Park.

Back Atop the ACC

Eleven of Jerry Claiborne's players were selected in the 1975 NFL draft, the most since 1951, when a school-record 12 players were picked.

That did not stop Maryland from repeating as ACC champs in 1975 and 1976. From 1974 to 1976, Maryland did not lose one ACC game.

Two games, intertwined by the initial failure, and then the ultimate success of placekicker Mike Sotchko, defined Maryland's 1975 season.

The 14th-ranked Terps sported a 4-1-1 record before playing ninth-ranked Penn State in November 1 in College Park. Maryland had never beaten the Nittany Lions. Defensive miscues helped cause a 24-17 loss at State College the previous season. "We knew we had the opportunity and the team to compete with them in 1976," said quarterback Mark Manges.

In front of 58,973 spectators, the largest crowd to watch a Maryland football game at home, the Terps fell behind 12-0. Manges started the first two games that season at quarterback. But he separated a shoulder in the second game against Tennessee and did not play that position until subbing in for starter Larry Dick late in the first quarter against Penn State. Dick had thrown an interception, and Maryland had also lost a fumble.

"Jerry [Claiborne], God rest his soul, had a quick hook for quarterbacks," said Manges.

Maryland pulled ahead 13-12 in the second half, and then the Nittany Lions kicked a field goal to make it 15-13 with six minutes left.

Maryland drove down the field to Penn State's 25-yard line with one minute remaining and was forced to try a field goal from the right hash mark.

Manges was the holder for Sotchko. "When he hit it, I looked up and saw it was going to the right upright. About 10 yards out, it floated to the right. We still laugh today that Route 1 would have been closed down if he had made that kick."

Manges said Maryland was a deflated team when they won the next game against Cincinnati by just two points.

"We were battling; we had two losses and a tie," said Manges. "We were just trying to make a bowl game. At that time, there were about half as many bowl games as there are now. That made the next game against Clemson so big. A loss would have meant no bowl game."

Manges had lost his starting job again after a poor performance in the Cincinnati game. Against Clemson, he replaced Dick at quarterback in the third quarter with Maryland behind, 20-12. Maryland scored a touchdown and then faced another last-minute field goal, this one from 40 yards on the hash mark in the center of the field.

Although eerily similar to the last-minute kick against Penn State, there was one major difference. Starting center Gene Ochap was injured on the previous play. In the huddle, as Sotchko was off to the side preparing for the kick, Manges looked up and surprisingly saw the seldom-used backup center Jack Sharkey across from him. There was mild concern.

"It all happened so fast, we didn't know Gene was hurt," said Manges. "With Jack, the snap could have gone anywhere. Deep snapping was not his forte. All year long, coaches in practice were yelling at him to 'concentrate on the hands, hit the hands.' When I saw him in the huddle, I said, 'Jack,' he said, 'I know, Mark, hit the hands.'"

Sharkey snapped the ball right to Manges's hands, and Sotchko split the uprights with the kick.

"When we came in the locker room, after the game, we all just looked at each other and said, 'Man I hope we didn't just blow it,' for a bowl game. We not only had to win, but we had to be impressive. It wasn't jubilation, but complete relief."

Maryland secured a bid to the Gator Bowl the next week after gaining 802 all-purpose yards, a Maryland football record, in a 62-24 win over Virginia. A 13-0 win over Florida in the Gator Bowl followed.

Almost a Dream Season

Manges stayed healthy in 1976 and started all 12 games for a team that he said "was full of studs."

They included defensive tackle Joe Campbell, an All-American that season; defensive back Kenny Roy and linebacker Brad Carr; tailbacks Steve Atkins, George Scott and Alvin "Preacher" Maddox; and fullback Tim Wilson.

"We were so good that year that from the first game, we went from a snap count of one on every play," said Manges. "We never changed a play."

Maryland rolled through its first 11 games unbeaten, suffering a scare only against a weak Wake Forest team in a game of which Manges said "we were just flat that day."

Even an injury to starting back Atkins, who ran for 120 yards in the Gator Bowl against Florida the year before as a freshman, in the fifth game against NC State could not derail the Terps. "We were deep on both sides of the ball," said Manges. "Atkins's injury didn't hurt us at all."

Scott and Maddox stepped in dutifully for Atkins. But the big difference, says Mangus, was the play of fullback Tim Wilson.

"The key to our offense was Tim Wilson," said Manges. "Anytime we ran the tailback, he was the lead blocker. On our sprint-option, he would lead the tailback to the outside. We ran a sprint out pass often. He would put that defensive end on the ground every time. His isolation blocks on the linebacker would open holes. If we had lost him, we would have fallen off a bit."

Manges says the biggest game during that regular season was against Kentucky in College Park in late October. "We had been losing mostly to Southeastern Confence teams," he said. "They were strong. But we dominated them. The defense shut them down after the first quarter."

Kentucky scored first to go up 7-0; then the defense, led by Joe Campbell's 22 tackles, took over, and Maryland won 24-14. Three shutouts later, the fourth-rated Terps played in the Cotton Bowl on New Year's Day against Houston.

"We came out a little star-struck," said Manges. This time, the defense struggled, giving up 320 rushing yards to Houston. By the end of the first quarter, Maryland was behind 21-0. Maryland lost 30-21. Manges and Wilson scored on runs and Manges connected on another score with tight end Eric Sievers, and Maryland trailed 27-21 with just under nine minutes remaining. But Houston ran almost six minutes off the clock and converted a field goal to secure the win. It was Maryland's only appearance in the Cotton Bowl.

Boomer's Bold Moves

After Ralph Friedgen accepted the job as an offensive coordinator for Bobby Ross, Friedgen called outgoing head coach Jerry Claiborne, for whom Friedgen had worked as a graduate assistant in the early 1970s.

Claiborne told Friedgen that Maryland really had one quarterback, Stan Gelbaugh. So Friedgen was surprised when he saw how well Frank Reich and Boomer Esiason threw the ball during Ross's first spring football practice in 1982.

"I thought we had a chance to be really good with three guys who could throw the ball so well," said Freidgen. "When Boomer

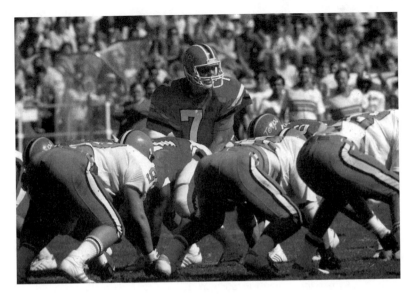

Boomer Esiason

threw the ball, I actually heard the ball whistle through the air. I couldn't believe it."

Esiason was an All-State quarterback his senior year for East Islip High School in Long Island, New York, but received only one offer to play football. Wake Forest sent him a letter, saying he was a "diamond in the rough." But Esiason did not hear from the school after receiving the letter.

Esiason also played varsity basketball and baseball at East Islip and had strongly considered an offer to pitch for St. John's University in Queens, New York.

But after assistant coach Tom Groom saw Esiason play basketball at East Islip while scouting another player, he lured Boomer to play football for Maryland. It was the only football scholarship offer he received.

Esiason played several positions with Maryland's junior varsity his freshman year, including quarterback, kicker, punter, safety and punt returner. His only experience in a varsity game was when he dressed as a "zingo," an underclassman not on the varsity roster who dressed for a varsity game, Esiason thought he was good enough to play varsity that year.

"I was an unchained tiger in a cage when I got to Maryland," said Esiason.

Esiason also admits he was not the most grounded freshman. "Early on I figured I was the best player on the team, and I let people know about it," he said.

Esiason laughs when he recalls how he was a victim of a hazing ritual performed on such full-of-themselves freshman. To quell the unrealistic ambitions of such rookies, veteran players lured the victim out into the dormitory hall by ringing the phone near their room and saying the victim had a phone call.

"I was a dumbass and came out," said Esiason.

The veterans quickly placed a wool hat over Esiason's head and face, stripped him naked and taped his hands and ankles behind his back. They placed him in an elevator on the seventh or eight floor of the Ellicott residential dorm and pushed a button for the first floor.

"Funny, Tom Groom was the guy who first saw me when I got down to the first floor," said Esiason. "I must admit they did it to the most deserving guy at the time. It was degrading. But I promised I would never do that to anyone."

The disappointment of redshirting his sophomore year put Esiason into such a state of despair that he nearly flunked out of school. He was forced to take and pass classes in summer school before the next season to remain eligible.

The only action Esiason saw the first game of the season was holding for the placekicker. He was not happy. "I was so pissed after that game," said Esiason. "I was a little loopy then and in some ways I regret it because it made me a little tough to be around. But it also made me the way I am. You can't accept failure."

I asked Esiason what got him through that time in his Maryland career. "I was afraid of failure," he said. "And when my dad was alive, I didn't want to disappoint him. I came damn close, though."

After quarterback Brent Dewitz injured a knee in the Vanderbilt game, Claiborne opted to start Esiason, a third-stringer behind Dewitz and Bob Milkovich the next week against West

Virginia. Milkovich missed the game due to bruised ribs. On his first play of the game, Esiason was sacked for 15 yards, a play he said then would cause him nightmares. He completed 15 of 32 passes and threw two interceptions in the game. Maryland finished 4-6-1 in Claiborne's last season, but Esiason set a Maryland record for completions in a season with 122.

Esiason's arm strength and leadership propelled him to the starting job the following fall for the Terps, and helped him keep the job for two seasons. "Boomer is a born leader and a streaky player," said Friedgen. "After Boomer would came off the field after he just threw seven incompletions, I'd say, 'What's going on?' He'd say, 'Relax, coach, I'm just warming up.' Then he'd go out and complete 10 in a row."

During a home game against Miami in 1982, there was some confusion among Ross, Friedgen and assistant coach Joe Krivak, as well as Esiason, as they discussed a two-point conversion following a touchdown that put them within four of Miami midway through the fourth quarter.

"Boomer said, 'I got it, I got it.' I asked, "What's the play?' Ross said, 'Hell if I know." We called a drop-back pass, and Boomer hit Mike Lewis for the conversion. His innovation and confidence won that game."

Esiason said that was not the first time he had reacted that way in that situation. "I had done that before," said Esiason. "If somebody was all wacked out on the field, I would say, 'I got it, leave me alone.' I had to make them think I knew what I was doing all the time."

The conversion made the score 17-15 in favor of Miami. Jess Atkinson later won the game with a 38-yard field goal with 2:14 left. Miami missed a 40-yarder with 12 seconds remaining in the game.

The next year, Esiason's senior season, provided a fond memory of the quarterback's Maryland career. A sprained right shoulder prevented Esiason from playing in the third game against Pittsburgh at Byrd Stadium. That allowed Reich, his roommate who was a year behind Boomer, to start his first game for the Terps. Esiason says Maryland recruited Reich in part because they thought Esiasion was going to flunk out of school.

It was a profound way for Reich, who was raised in the Pittsburgh area, to start his Maryland career. After home games, Esiason had a ritual of throwing a ball into the stands. Although Esiason did not play in the Pitt game, he asked Reich to join him in the postgame ritual.

Esiason returned to the starting lineup the next game against Virginia and helped lead Maryland into the Citrus Bowl, which they lost to Tennessee. The first installment of Quarterback U at Maryland had been completed. At Maryland, Esiason is second in career passing touchdowns (42), passing yards (6259) and passing completions (461) and is third in touchdowns in a seasons with 18. Esiason later played with three NFL teams from 1984 to 1997 and led the Bengals to the Super Bowl. Fortunately for Ross, Frank Reich and Stan Gelbaugh remained after Esiason's departure.

Cirovski Revives Soccer Program

When Sasho Cirovski was seeking the men's soccer head coach's job at Maryland in the early 1990s, he asked for a copy of the sport's media guide to research the history of the program. He was told he would receive one in the mail. He never did. Cirovski says the school media rep who promised to send him the guide later told him he was embarrassed to admit that there was no media guide for the sport.

"Soccer had become a sport that was just purely surviving," said Cirovski, who took over the program in 1993. The team had won just 10 games in its previous two seasons. After the first season ended at 3-14-1, Cirovski quickly turned the program around. In 1996, Maryland won the ACC Tournament for the first time. with a team that Cirovski says was his best at Maryland. Senior captain Shane Dougherty, second in career points at Maryland and Cirovski's first recruit, scored a goal in the championship game, a 2-0 win over Virginia.

"That was the turning point of the program, when we became a national presence," said Cirovski.

Maryland reached the NCAA Final Four in 1998 and 2002. In 2002, Maryland set a school record with 20 wins and were 13-

0 at home, including a compelling 3-0 NCAA tournament quarterfinal win over Connecticut.

The Huskies, national champions in 2000, were not the only formidable foe confronting the Terps in that game. College Park endured a crippling snowstorm the week prior to the game. Cirovski convinced the school's grounds crew to plow the field for almost two consecutive days to keep the field clear. "They did it out of respect for the program," said Cirovksi. "The field was perfect, it was dry as could be."

Also, the women's soccer team, coached by Cirovski's wife Shannon, volunteered their time by clearing snow off the bleachers the day of the game. All the work enabled 3,460 chilled fans to attend the game surrounded by five-foot-high snowbanks. It was the largest crowd to watch a postseason game at Ludwig Field and the second largest in history.

Dominic Mediate scored all four of the Terps' postseason goals up to that point, including two in the win over Connecticut. Maryland entered the NCAA tournament semifinal against UCLA as the top ranked team in the country, but they fell to the Bruins, 2-1.

24

The Tenacity of
Tyler and Her Troops

The Tenacity of Tyler and Her Troops

For a time, the women's lacrosse and field hockey teams were forced to use mobile locker rooms. A truck with a Maryland logo emblazoned on the outside served as equipment room and part-time locker room for the teams in the late 1970s to 1988.

Coaches drove the utility vehicle, known as "The Bread Truck," to wherever the team practiced or played games on campus.

Sue Tyler was the matron of women's lacrosse and field hockey at Maryland. She was the head coach of both teams from 1974 until 1987 and won NCAA titles in lacrosse in 1981 and 1986 and field hockey in 1987.

Tyler speaks fondly of the multi-use vehicle. "There was one seat for the driver and a broken seat for the passenger, and an open space in the back for equipment and the players to change," she said.

"One year, the side door broke off. We hoped nobody would steal our equipment."

After the truck stopped working, the coaches and players were forced to store their equipment in the trunks of their cars. Eventually, the teams were allowed to use the visiting team locker room in Cole Field House, when it was available.

Tyler often used her own push lawnmower to cut the field's grass and make it playable. She used most of the team's money to support trips out of state, leaving no money for recruiting. "I rarely recruited," she said. "They asked me why I wanted to go so far. I told them that's where the best teams were."

Tyler had to make some sacrifices to practice on the football team's Astroturf field. She says Jerry Claiborne, the football team's head coach, refused to give the team a key to enter the field, which was surrounded by a fence. Undeterred, the team climbed through a drainpipe to get to the field.

Tyler remembers some profound moments from her coaching days. One of her two-sport athletes, Denise Westcott, was the first recipient of a women's athletic scholarship at Maryland.

Not all women athletes welcomed scholarships. Tyler remembers how a group of female and male athletes staged a parade on campus to protest Title IX, a federal law signed in 1972 that requires equal treatment for women in collegiate athletics.

"They thought it would commercialize athletics," said Tyler. "They also though money shouldn't go to athletic scholarships while teams had no uniforms and were traveling to competitions by private car."

Today, both the women's lacrosse and field hockey teams receive the full allotment of scholarships. The field hockey team has created 30 All-Americans and has won five ACC titles, its first coming in 1992.

Ross Takes Over

Dick Dull had never worked as an athletic director before he assumed that post at Maryland on August 3, 1981 at the age of 35. His first big task was finding a new football coach after Jerry Claiborne resigned following the 1981 season to take the head coaching job at Kentucky.

Dull said the school's chancellor, Dr. John Slaughter, let Dull pick Claiborne's successor on his own. There was no search committee. "He said,'You're going to pick the coach, and I'm going to approve it,'" said Dull.

Dull solicited the advice of former Maryland quarterback Jack Scarbath, who, along with sports information director Jack Zane, told Dull the best candidate for the job was Bobby Ross, an assistant coach with the Kansas City Chiefs.

Ross, who had been an assistant under Claiborne in 1972, thought his chances of getting the job were not very good. "I had heard the job was going to a big-time guy," he said. "I wasn't a big-time guy."

After a six-week search, Dull chose Ross. "I wanted someone who would represent the institution in a positive manner," he said. "And I wanted someone who would create exciting, attacking football. I knew that defense wins games but offense sell tickets."

At the press conference introducing Ross as Maryland's new football coach, a blond-haired sophomore quarterback stood among the crowd.

"One of the big things I was hearing was there was a big left-handed quarterback on the team," said Ross. "Everybody said he had a tremendous amount of talent. I was looking for him at the press conference."

The quarterback, Boomer Esiason, listened intently as Ross spoke of designing an offense that featured a more diverse attack. It was a drastic change compared to Claiborne.

"It was as vanilla as it got with Claiborne," said Esiason. "Run right, run left, run up the middle, punt and play good defense. But there's no question Jerry made me a tougher player because of how he expected the quarterback to be. We were getting hit in practice. We never wore a yellow or red jersey. We'd do drills where the quarterbacks had to take on linebacker. It was like he had a sign place on our back, 'Hit us, we're stupid.' It made you a tougher player."

After the press conference, Esiason sought out Dull and congratulated him for selecting Ross as the new coach.

"During the conference, Bobby said 'I'm going to install a pro-style offense and throw the ball downfield,'" said Esiason. "I'm like, 'Oh my God, this is the best thing I've ever heard.' I couldn't wait to give Dick Dull a kiss."

Ross Loosens the Reins

Soon after taking the Maryland job, Ross noticed Maryland's players were uncomfortable with their living situations.

"Their biggest complaint was they wanted to get out of the seventh and eight floors [of their dorm]," said Ross. "I wanted to get them out of there. I wanted to treat them as grown men."

Claiborne, a stern disciplinarian, placed all players on the two floors. Ralph Larry remembers how the team's academic advisor lived with the players in the dorm to ensure players didn't break the rules.

"If you missed curfew during the season, you had to run around the campus with [the advisor] at 5:30 in the morning. It seemed like that happened every day."

Ross moved the players to dorms on the south part of campus. They lived among other students. "I felt like [in Ellicott] there were caged lions," he said. "They were small rooms. I stayed up there for a while when I was an assistant coach. I wanted out of there real quick. Players probably perceived me as less disciplined, but I didn't feel that way. You have to build a program on bond and trust."

Ross instituted a curfew during the season and placed an assistant to live among some of the players. But his approach was more congenial than punitive. "I'd go by on Thursday night during the season and visit with the guys" he said. "I never really checked them much. I wanted them to feel comfortable with us as people."

Taming the Tar Heels, Trouble with the Tigers

Ross lost his first two games, against Penn State and by a point to West Virginia, both on the road. "I thought we were doing well," said Ross. "We had a chance to win both games. I always believed in being positive."

The Terps then won their next seven games, including a critical contest against 10th-ranked North Carolina. With the Terps behind at halftime, offensive lineman Dave Pacella, a senior captain, stood up and banged his helmet into a locker. He loudly insisted that Maryland needed to run the ball more often.

"I said, 'Okay, we're going to run the ball,'" said Ross. "'We'll put this game in the hands of the offensive linemen.' I felt instinctively that was what we should do."

In the second half, running back Willie Joyner broke touchdown runs of 49 and 84 yards on the way to a 240-yard rushing day, the third longest one game total in Maryland history. The 31-24 Terps win placed them at 4-0 in the ACC, with games remaining against Clemson and Virginia. But two weeks later, the Terps lost by two points to Clemson at home. The Terps ended the season the next week with a comfortable win over Virginia, and its fourth second place conference finish in five years.

Maryland played its first game under lights in Byrd Stadium the following season, in front of 54,715 fans. The 17th ranked Terps suffered a 10-point loss to West Virginia in the second game of the season. The Terps then won five in a row and were ranked 13th when third-ranked North Carolina came to College Park. Maryland beat the Tar Heels for the second consecutive season, this time by two points on a 30-yard pass from Esiason to Sean Sullivan. Ross called the win in front of 51,200 fans one of his biggest thrills.

Again, the Terps walked away from a Carolina game unbeaten in conference play. And again, Clemson loomed two weeks later, this time in South Carolina. Clemson, ranked 17th, crushed the 11th ranked Terps 52-27 in front of 81,000 fans in Death Valley "We were humiliated," said Ross. "We just didn't show up that day."

Ross admittedly made things worse with a postgame comment to a reporter that referred to Clemson's probation for recruiting violations. "After the game, a reporter asked me if I could explain why we played so bad. I said, 'Yeah, I've got 178 reasons.' I was young and mad and we had gotten beat real bad. It was not the right thing to say."

Clemson was unbeaten against ACC opponents that year, but could not claim the title because it was on probation. Despite losing to Clemson, Maryland won the ACC title when Virginia upset North Carolina the same day.

Another Loss to the Nittany Lions

In 1984, Maryland was a young team with instability at quarterback for the first time in Ross's three-year career. The Terps had ended the 1983 season ranked 17th in the country after losing to Tennessee in the Florida Citrus Bowl.

The youth showed early. For the second time under Ross, the Terps started the season with two losses. Ross says Keeta Covington's 47-yard punt return in the second quarter in the third game against 17th-ranked West Virginia was one of the key plays of the entire season. It led to the game's first touchdown.

"We were a different team after that punt," he said. "It gave us some confidence."

Maryland won the game 20-17 after Jess Atkinson kicked a 20-yard field goal with 21 seconds remaining and were 2-2 when they faced 11th-ranked Penn State two weeks later in front of 85,456 fans in State College.

Frank Reich had started the first four games for Maryland, but separated his throwing shoulder in the win over Wake Forest. Junior Stan Gelbaugh, Maryland's punter and a career backup at quarterback, started behind center against Penn State the next week and nearly led the Terps to an upset over the 11th-ranked Nittany Lions.

Trailing 25-24, Gelbaugh completed a pass to Sean Sullivan that placed the Terps at Penn State's 35 yard-line with four seconds left. With no timeouts, Ross yelled from the sideline for Gelbaugh to "kill" the ball, meaning the quarterback should throw the ball out of bounds to stop the clock. In that case, Maryland would have 25 seconds to set up Jess Atkinson to kick a possible game-winning 52-yard field goal.

But as Gelbaugh was behind center to begin the play, he saw Atkinson running onto the field, and he ran off the field. In the confusion, holder Dan Henning took the snap and threw it out of bounds. But some Maryland players were not set, and Maryland was penalized five yards. With one second left, Atkinson was pacing off his steps preparing for the field goal attempt. Then, suddenly, the game was over, as was another Maryland dream to beat Penn State.

The tough loss to the Nittany Lions did not stifle the Terps. They won their next three games against ACC opponents and were 4-0 in conference play. One was a 34-23 win over North Carolina. After the game, Maryland assistant coach Ralph Friedgen said hello to Reich's father.

"He was upset," said Friedgen. "I can remember him saying, 'Is Frank well?' I said, 'Yeah.' He said, 'Don't you have a rule where if your starting quarterback is not hurt, you play him?' I said, 'Yeah, but Stan is hot. You're speaking like a father. We can't make the change. I can tell you this, Frank's going to have to come in and win a football game for us.' The next game was against Miami. I asked him, 'Are you going to the Miami game?' He said, 'No.' I said, 'I'm sorry to hear that. We're going to need Frank before this thing is all over.' "

Miracle in Miami

The week before the Miami game, Reich approached Ross and told him he was ready to play. Ross told him Gelbaugh was still the starting quarterback.

"He said, 'I thought starters return when they're healthy.' I said, "Normally they do, but our team's won five in a row. I can't make that change.' He said, 'What do I have to do? I said, 'Be ready. You're one play from going in.'"

Ross decided to put Reich in the game when he walked to the locker room at halftime with the Terps behind 31-0 to the sixth-ranked Hurricanes.

"I didn't like anything we were doing," said Ross. "I couldn't blame it on our offense. [Miami quarterback] Bernie Kosar was just picking us apart. I felt like we were playing on ice. We were very tentative. I thought we were intimidated. They had run through our warmup before the game, hollering and screaming and cussing."

Ross made a couple of tactical changes at halftime. To prevent wasting time, he stopped the motion shifting before the snap and told his offensive players to move quicker in and out of the huddle. And he took out all special coverage on defense, using basic coverages instead.

He also leveled a threat. "I told them that if we don't play well in the second half, they won't go back to their girlfriends. They'll run a 40-yard dash for every point they score."

Maryland kicked off to start the second half, but on Miami's opening possession Scott Schankweiler intercepted a Miami pass, setting up a Greg Hill touchdown. Maryland scored on its first six possessions.

"After our third touchdown, [assistant coach] George Foussekis walked past me, and I said, 'George, we can win this game now,'" said Ross. "I've never seen momentum change like that. You can't really explain it. It just happens. We had a lot of prideful guys. Frank [Reich] came in and ran a wonderfully tempoed game."

Reich completed 12 of 15 passes for 260 yards and three touchdowns. Maryland took the lead for the first time on a 68-yard pass from Reich to Greg Hill. Miami safety Darrell Fullington got both hands on the pass, but the ball slid off his fingers and into Hill's hands.

Miami then fumbled Maryland's kickoff, and Rick Badanjek scored on a four-yard run to put the Terps up 42-34.

With little more than one minute remaining, Kosar threw a touchdown pass to cut Maryland's lead to two points. The Hurricanes then missed the two-point conversion. Maryland cornerback Joe Kraus recovered Miami's onside kick and returned it to Miami's one-yard line. Friedgen, the offensive coordinator, then called a quarterback sneak and Maryland moved the ball to the one-yard line.

That did not please Ross. "Bobby said, 'What are doing, Ralph? If we score they get the ball back. Kill the ball,'" said Friedgen. "So we killed the clock."

Maryland players said after the game that the Miami players taunted the Terps in the first half, saying, "Come on, Maryland, at least make it close." Kraus said after the game the Miami players would not congratulate the Terps. Miami coach Jimmy Johnson called the loss "The most disappointing he had ever been associated with."

One person happy to see the result was Tony Edwards, Maryland's left offensive tackle, who injured a knee in the first half. Edwards had showered and stayed in the locker room to listen to the game on his headset, thinking the Terps had no chance to win. He tried to return to the field when Maryland stormed back, but found he had been locked in. Edwards reached Maryland's sideline just as the game had ended.

Overwhelmed by Maryland's unlikely triumph, Maryland linebacker Chuck Faucette passed out on the bench after game. Amid the postgame jubilation on the field, one of Maryland's co-captains, Kevin Glover, picked up Ross and held him in a bear hug. "He said, 'Coach, do we still have to run those 40s?' I said, 'No, Kevin, you don't have to do that.'"

Revenge in Baltimore

The Terps were still unranked when they faced Clemson the next week in Baltimore. Sixty thousand fans crowded Memorial Stadium in the first Terp football game played in Charm City.

Clemson upped the game's emotional ante two weeks before the game on the tarmac at Raleigh-Durham International Airport. Maryland's football team was sitting in a plane on the runway waiting to take off and return to College Park after its win over North Carolina. A plane with the Clemson players was also taxiing on the tarmac, preparing to take off to Columbia, South Carolina after its game against NC State.

Although Clemson was unbeaten against ACC teams that season, it could not officially claim the title since it was on probation. Still, the school purchased rings symbolic of the triumph.

As Clemson's plane passed Maryland's plane on the runway, some of the Tigers held their rings at their windows, taunting the Maryland players.

"I told one of the coaches, 'We won't have to say much to those guys to get them ready for that game,'" said Ross.

Ross stopped by some of the players' rooms on Thursday night before the Saturday evening game. When he walked into the room occupied by center Kevin Glover and offensive lineman Leonard Lynch, he saw two throwing darts stuck in a life size poster of William "The Refrigerator" Perry, Clemson's 340-pound middle guard who lined up opposite Glover.

On November 17, Maryland gained 577 yards and beat Clemson 41-23 after falling behind 23-17 early in the second half.

Alvin Blount rushed for 214 yards and Reich threw for 177 yards. After the game outside the locker room, Friedgen ran into Frank Reich's father, who had decided to not attend Maryland's game against Miami the week before.

"He says, 'Where's your crystal ball?'" said Friedgen. "I said, 'You missed the game of a lifetime. I knew it was going to happen.'"

Maryland clinched the ACC title for the second consecutive year after beating Virginia the following week. Typical of the season, the 12th-ranked Terps mounted another dramatic second-half comeback to beat Tennessee, 28-27, in the Sun Bowl after falling behind by 21 points at halftime.

Badanjek scored the winning touchdown with just more than two minutes to play. On the ensuing series of plays for Tennessee, Keeta Covington forced a Tennessee fumble deep in Maryland's territory, erasing a possible field goal attempt by the Volunteers. The ball was recovered by Covington's brother, Al.

It was Maryland's first bowl victory in five tries since 1977.

Same Fate vs. State

Maryland football reached a pinnacle of sorts with Bobby Ross as head coach when it received a number one preseason ranking by *Sport Magazine* in 1985. The Associated Press ranked the Terps number seven, 12 positions ahead of the season's first opponent, Penn State. Maryland faced its best chance of beating the Nittany Lions for only the second time in 25 tries. Maryland last beat Penn State 21-17 in 1961.

More than 50, 000 fans attended the contest in College Park on September 7. Maryland started the game ominously, giving up an interception that led to a Penn State score on their first possession. Quarterback Stan Gelbaugh threw two more interceptions in the game. In the last minute of the game and down by two points, Maryland, dropped a pass and then lost the ball after a fumble on the same series of downs inside Penn State's 24-yard line. And new placekicker Ramon Paredes missed two field goals in the fourth quarter. Penn State continued its curse over the Terps, winning 20-18.

Still, Maryland repeated as ACC champions for the second consecutive season, helped by another dramatic win over Clemson late in the season.

Maryland was 4-0 in the conference going into the Clemson clash in South Carolina on November 16. And for the first time during the Ross era, the Terps faced an unranked Tigers team.

Aided by a Saturday morning pregame pep rally in the stadium attended by 65,000 fans, Clemson started strong and went ahead 10-0. But Maryland fought back and tied the game in the final minutes when Stan Gelbaugh threw a three-yard pass to Ferrel Edmunds for the score, tying the game at 31. Gelbaugh threw for 361 yards, breaking Esiason's two-year old record of 355 in one game.

After the play, Clemson coach Danny Ford ran onto the field to complain to the referees that the score should not count. First, he claimed the 25-second clock ran out before Maryland hiked the ball. Second, he thought Edmunds, who quickly threw the ball to the ground, did not possess the ball long enough for a score.

"That got the crowd all riled up," said Ross.

Maryland got the ball back with just under a minute to play, and Gellbaugh charged the Terps down deep into Clemson territory. Stan Plocki kicked the game-winning field goal from 20 yards with three seconds to play.

On Maryland's kickoff, Ross said players on the Clemson bench pulled down a Maryland player running near the Clemson sideline and started beating on him. A fight erupted on the field, hindering Maryland's celebration for clinching at least a tie for the ACC title. A win over Virginia two weeks later clinched the conference crown for Maryland.

It would also be the last time a Maryland football team would be ranked in the nation's top 20 until 2001.

Rough Sendoff for Ross

Ironically, the only season Maryland started off with three wins in Ross's five year career, 1986, was the year they performed poorly in the ACC. Maryland lost its first two conference matches, to NC State and Wake Forest.

The week before another grueling contest with Clemson, Maryland lost by two points to Penn State. In Ross's head coaching career with Maryland, his teams lost to Penn State by two points twice and by one point once.

The game against 15th-ranked Clemson at Baltimore's Memorial Stadium featured a low point in Ross's Maryland career. Maryland held a three-point lead over Clemson with about two minutes remaining. The scoreboard showed one timeout for Clemson as they tried to march into Terp territory. After they called a timeout, Ross said he checked with an official to make sure Clemson was out of timeouts. He said the official confirmed that fact.

Maryland set up in a prevent defense, figuring Clemson would have to pass the ball. When Clemson started running the ball, Ross figured something was wrong. Then Clemson called a time out at Maryland's 11-yard line. The officials let the timeout stand, allowing Clemson to set up for a field goal, which they converted to tie the game.

As time ran out, an enraged Ross ran frantically onto the field to confront the official who told him Clemson had no time outs remaining. But the cord on Ross's headset ran out and he was jerked to a stop. He never reached the official.

"I was going to look him in the eye and tell him that I was going to report him for giving me wrong information," said Ross.

Maryland ended the season with a 42-10 win over Virginia. Unknown to Ross and the players at the time, it would be Ross's last game as Maryland's head coach.

No Regrets for Ross

Many of Bobby Ross's family members attended the last Maryland football game of the 1986 season against Virginia in Charlottesville. Despite the Terps' commanding 42-10 win, the mood on the ride home for Ross, his wife and four of his five children was far from celebratory. It was during that two and a half-hour ride that the Ross family talked much about Dad's coaching future. They decided that Ross would step down as Maryland's head coach.

Toward the end of the season, Ross met with acting athletic director Charles Sturtz to discuss the future of Maryland athletics following the death of Len Bias. That was a big step for Ross, who admittedly tried to avoid such meetings with athletic administrators because he thought it might build up resentment among professors and other school officials. "I don't think that was my job as a football coach," he said.

In the meeting, Ross wanted clarifications about Maryland's admissions policy, which was being scrutinized following Bias's death. He was told it could be as long as three or four years. "That's when I started to think about it," said Ross. "Not having a defined direction and all the other distractions, I felt it was time to move one."

There were plenty of distractions. His good friend, athletic director Dick Dull, had resigned under pressure in October. Another good friend, men's basketball coach Lefty Driesell, had resigned in September. Further, Ross said his players were constantly bombarded by the media to talk about the fallout from the Bias death. Ross said school administrators told him he had to let his players talk to the media. Comparatively little was asked about the football team.

"It didn't help that we were the first team to play a season after his death," said Ross. "I would get questions that weren't asking about the next game or opponent. Guys would constantly come up to me and ask what they should say. I told them to tell the truth. It was a big distraction."

Ross places some blame on those distractions for Maryland's 5-5-1 season, one that he said started with expectations "probably equal" to any other team he coached at Maryland. Ross claims injuries to key players, including to running back Tommy Neal, also contributed to his worst season at Maryland.

Ross said he told his players shortly after the season that he resigned because he felt "at that time, they needed a change and I needed a change. The media talked a lot about poor facilities being a big deal. I would have liked better facilities, but that wasn't the reason. There was no athletic director who was going to give me better answers for the long range and short term."

Two months after resigning from Maryland, Ross accepted the job as head coach at Georgia Tech. At the end of 1990, the football coaches' poll voted the Yellow Jackets the top team in the country. They shared the national title with Colorado.

After leaving Tech, Ross coached five years with the San Diego Chargers, taking them to the Super Bowl, and five more years with the Detroit Lions. He now resides in rural Virginia.

Reflections

Like most sports-obsessed youth, I wanted to be a professional athlete, more specifically a basketball player. I wanted to be the next great point guard, just like Terp guard Brad Davis, who ran the court with controlled abandon, his blonde hair flopping around like a golden mop atop a bouncing stick.

I remember vividly the many games Maryland's basketball team played on national television in the early 1970s. Two things impressed me most profoundly—the energetic play of Brad Davis and Maryland's home court at Cole Field House. What the hell was a Terrapin? I was intrigued.

I knew then that I wanted to go the University of Maryland and be the next Brad Davis. I achieved half of those goals.

I had already decided on attending Maryland before the track coach invited down to the school in the late spring of 1976 for a visit.

My visit to Maryland lasted three days, one day longer than anticipated, so that I could stay and watch the U.S.A.-Russia dual track meet at Byrd Stadium. I stayed in the dorm rooms in Byrd Stadium's north building, on the second floor above the visiting football locker room and the track office.

What the cramped room lacked in comfort it made up for in functionality. It was like living in a big box. That building would be my home for two and a half years and would be the largest portion of my partial scholarship. And I cherished those moments.

Once during the visit, I sat on the grass inside the stadium and marveled at its grand wonder. Although capacity was about 45,000, the stadium looked like the Roman Coliseum for a boy from central New Jersey. I savored the environment and dreamed of running record times on the track that surrounded the football field.

My fantasies were interrupted by a swift-moving man running laps vigorously counterclockwise on the track. It was Marty Liquori, who was there to work as an analyst for the television broadcast of the track meet the next day. Liquori, also a New Jersey native, was a running idol when I grew up.

When he started to run onto the track, I leaped off the grass and hustled over to him as he slowed to a jog. I introduced myself and asked for his autograph. As he signed, I asked him, "Working hard, eh?"

Sweat dripping from his brow, Liquori calmly said, "No, getting an easy one in today." And then he was off. A few minutes later, I peeled off my shirt and started running laps on the track, still wearing a pair of long corduroy pants.

The discomfort was irrelevant. I dreamed of running like Marty Liquori, of setting records on this track, which would be my new training grounds for the next few years. I tried to run as fast as Liquori had done, only I was working much harder. Could it get any better?

I worked several jobs during my days in Terpland, as part of my scholarship. Some were enjoyable and even challenging—ushering football and basketball games, selling football season tickets during the summer between my junior and senior years. Others were tedious and easy, like checking student identification at the entrances of the school recreation centers.

My final job my senior year was the easiest and ultimately the most adventurous. I was the dorm monitor for the front rooms at Ritchie Coliseum for about $50 a month. In that role, I was to ensure my fellow students practiced proper student decorum (good luck enforcing that one, even if I knew what it was) and keeping the halls clean. I generally ignored the first responsibility. As for the second one, I ignored that, too.

After my first month on the job, some of my fellow dorm mates—all track athletes—started to complain about the unkempt environment.

"Relax, I'll get to it," I'd say. After two months, I actually started to notice the dust balls and dirt starting to accumulate. Still, it wasn't enough for me to perform my duties.

By the third month, my dorm mates had lost patience with my indifference. They decided to try and shock me into submission. The wrestlers who lived in the back of Ritchie Coliseum occasionally hosted pig roasts on some weekends in the warmer months. After one joyous afternoon of such imbibing, I strolled back to my room for a nap. Imagine my surprise when I found a pig's head on my pillow, eyes open in a threatening stare. "Clean the damn dorm," it seemed to say. So much for the nap.

That shocking moment prompted me to finally clean the halls. But two months later, the halls returned to their familiar dirty state. The fellas had had enough.

While lounging in my room one early evening, I heard a yell from the bathroom at the end of the hall.

Something was happening on fraternity row, they said. I ran back to the bathroom along with several others and looked excitedly out the window that led to a fire escape. Moments later, several of the guys, led by 250-pound shot putter Dave Crimmins, grabbed me, held me to the ground, taped my hands and feet, and secured me with rope to a toilet.

"You gonna clean the halls?"

I grumbled profanities of denial.

"You gonna clean the halls?"

I continued to deny their request. They left me lying on the unsanitary bathroom floor to ponder their demand. After about a half-hour, I managed to break loose. As I walked back, humiliated and humbled, I cursed all those who had captured me. After a few days, though, I did clean the place.

Many more relaxing moments occurred in Ritchie as well. The venue was used for campus rock concerts and large mixers, often allowing us residents free entrance to the events. And you can bet we took advantage of the opportunity. Many times, we secured free admittance for many friends

It did not hurt that we had access to a balcony overlooking the arena floor from our hall, affording us prime seating for the events.

One room on our floor and most of the former storage rooms on the lower level were big enough to qualify as apartments. And many athletes converted the rooms into comfortable and large living quarters, with second floors and bars that they built themselves. Many supplies came from poorly secured construction sites.

The marquee suite was located on our floor, at one end of the hall. Most parties started and ended there, and for good reason. The room featured a bar, a metal spiral staircase that led to a loft for sleeping and lounging on couches and chairs, and its own bathroom.

On comfortable evenings, the parties flowed outside in front of the coliseum, prompting some spontaneous activity. Most memorable was when one of our pole vaulters, Neil Hughes, scaled the front of the building with his unequipped hands and feet. When he climbed to the roof, some 30 feet above ground, we responded with a round of applause. It was just another simple moment of joy at the Palace of Pleasure, Ritchie Coliseum.

By the early 1980s, athletes could no longer live in Ritchie Coliseum and Byrd Stadium. One ACC school complained Maryland had an unfair advantage placing athletes in those rooms because Maryland coaches did not have to pay for the rooms.

No longer could the track, baseball, wrestling, golf, tennis, lacrosse, and fencing teams place their athletes in those rooms. Even athletic trainers lived in Byrd Stadium. As a result, fewer scholarships were offered to athletes, affecting the performances of some of those teams.

Sprains, Pains, and Small Gains

My athletic career at Maryland could not have started much better. I scored a head ball off a corner kick in our first preseason soccer scrimmage. It didn't matter that I barely saw the ball and that it deflected off my nose. Without wearing glasses, I was close to legally blind. The glasses I usually wore to play soccer had broken, and the contact lenses I had ordered had not yet arrived.

A couple days later, I made the team as a walk-on. Then an ominous incident occurred. My right Achilles tendon flared up following a two-mile conditioning run before a preseason scrimmage in which I was scheduled to start as an outside attacker. My collegiate soccer career lasted less than one month.

I did not run for three months and spent a few weeks in a cast to isolate the tendon, jeopardizing my first year of track competition. I took out my frustration with aggressive weight conditioning and excessive beer drinking. Coupled with large amounts of processed school dining hall food, I gained 20 pounds my first semester away from home, going from 130 to 150.

I was miserable. Coming out of high school as a two-time soccer state champion as well an All-State soccer player and middle distance runner, I expected to make my hometown of Trenton, N.J. proud after my first season. I had run 1:53 as a high school half-miler. My goal was to break 1:50 my freshman year. I never broke 1:55. That summer, I went home to Trenton and worked in a factory, pulling wallboards off a large saw for eight hours a day. I wondered if my athletic career was over at the age of 19.

I knew where I had gone wrong. I was lazy during most of the summer before my freshman season, hanging out at the country club pool, playing golf and tennis, and caddying occasionally. I trained only sporadically for a couple weeks before I reported for soccer preseason camp. I created a situation where my body was likely to break down, and it did.

My sophomore season was injury-free, but I failed to reach my goal of breaking 1:50 again. After the first day of qualifying at the ACC outdoor meet, our ever-emotional coach, Frank Costello, walked down the aisle of our team bus, enthusiastically congratulating those who had qualified for the finals the next day. When he reached the back of the bus where my roommate and I, both non-qualifiers, sulked in our seats, Costello gave us a quick glance and said nothing before turning around and walking the other way to keep the rest of the troops pumped up. I was starting to feel like an athletic failure.

Then a summer living at the New Jersey beach with my siblings and working as a garbage man helped turn my career around. I spent most of the time working from 6 a.m. to 5 p.m., hauling heavy garbage bags and cans and then running on the beach. By the following fall season, I was stronger physically and mentally. Intense cross-country workouts were more focused the following fall. I finished third in the conference indoor 1000 meters and the conference outdoor 800 meters. I also finished sixth at the indoor IC4A conference 1000 meters and the outdoor 800 meters.

An incident in that meet showcased a personality trait that I feel prevented me from becoming a better runner. The IC4A was the largest conference in the U.S., with more than 100 schools from the Midwest to the northeast and Mid-Atlantic competing in just track and field and cross-country. Finishing among the leaders was considered an impressive accomplishment.

Early in the morning I had finished comfortably in the top four in a preliminary heat to qualify for the semifinal heats. Later that afternoon, in one semifinal, I was running comfortably in third place in the inside lane as we came off the final turn. The top four runners qualified for the next day's final.

A competitor trapped behind me then said, "Dave, move out." I had become friends with the runner, Billy Martin, from

Iona, and decided to do a friend a favor. My good deed almost cost me a place in the final.

When I gave Martin, a better half-miler than me by at least a couple seconds, some room, he quickly moved ahead into second place. I had to work hard the entire final stretch to barely hold off a runner for fourth place. I finished a disappointing sixth in the final the next day and fell about a second short of qualifying for the collegiate national meet, but I ran a personal best time.

That time was not improved upon my senior year. Shortly after the next indoor season, I developed tendinitis in my right ankle. The injury stemmed from two severe sprains of the ankle suffered in the fall. One came after hitting a hole on the school golf course during an easy recovery run following a cross country work out.

The other sprain was less noble. I interned in the sports promotions office of Maryland's athletic department during the fall semester that year. It happened during a touch football match between our staff and the department's broadcast syndication company. I initially refused, fearing injury.

But my boss persisted and I changed my mind, knowing I was violating a team rule not to participate in such an activity. While making a cut to the left on the Astroturf during a pass route, I misplanted my right foot and the ankle turned sharply. Two days later at a team meeting, Coach Costello rightfully made a point to single me out as an example of being an irresponsible captain. I missed valuable training time and endured a frustrating season.

At the beginning of the outdoor season, I developed severe tendinitis on the inside of the ankle and missed the entire season. Once I realized my fate, I spent six consecutive nights in a local bar drowning my sorrows. I could no longer attempt to qualify for the national collegiate outdoor meet and the Olympic trials, both attainable goals. My senior season was a bust. My track career certainly taught me how to deal with, and overcome, frustration and adversity.

Sinking Navy's Ship

There were some fond moments, though, mostly in my junior season. The Naval Academy was our most intense dual-meet rival during my years as a Terp. The battles created a high level of intensity and expectation.

The heightened level had been around since Jim Kehoe took over as Maryland head track coach in the 1950s. Kehoe often said to his troops, "The only thing better than beating Navy wis beating them twice."

Moments before our bus departed from College Park to head to Annapolis, the stern track statesman boarded the bus for a pre-meet pep talk. Kehoe's pep talks had the tone of a Patton speech, without the profanity. He could motivate a comatose cow to run a mile in three minutes

During his brief speech, Kehoe explained why it was so important to beat Navy, how our athletic lives depended on beating Navy, how the guys from Navy should not share the same breathing space with us, etc., etc. He made sure every bit of our manhood felt challenged. Lose to Navy, and we were not men.

Perhaps it was Kehoe's speech, but we dominated that meet, which also included Princeton. We beat Navy so badly—99 to 34 1/2—that their head coach, Jim Gehrdes, was seen after the meet sitting in solitary bewilderment in the bleachers, staring blankly into space, as if he had just seen the ghost of Kehoe's past.

The meet was one of the most rewarding of my career. I won the 800 meters and anchored the 4 x 800-meter relay team to a win, an effort coach Costello said in the *Diamondback* the next day was just as good as that of Renaldo Nehemiah, who had won three events.

Our most prominent outdoor conquest was at the ACC meet in Chapel Hill, North Carolina. Maryland had won the previous 24 conference outdoor meets and was not about to relinquish that dominant role. We projected ourselves with an air of confidence bordering on arrogance.

When the team departed the bus for the first day of competition, we walked together toward the bleachers. One athlete carried on his shoulder a boom box the size of a small suitcase that blared upbeat soul music. The team, some 40 strong, sang and strutted to the rhythm, covering our short walk with a sense of awkward assuredness—mostly uncoordinated distance runners mixing with ungraceful shot putters and discuss throwers and the smooth rhythms of the sprinters. It was the Average White Band merging with George Clinton and the P-Funk All-Stars. When we reached our destination point in the bleachers, the song stopped, as if to punctuate our arrival.

I had yet to qualify for the IC4A meet, the national collegiate meet and the Olympic trials, three goals that season. I finished third in a semifinal heat and qualified to run the final the next day. More importantly, the time had qualified me for the IC4A meet and was a personal best.

I finished fourth the next day, in another personal best, and contributed four points to our team's total. Later that year, the team had its best finish in school history at the NCAA outdoor meet.

THE BOOMER ESIASON FOUNDATION SALUTES THE MARYLAND TERRAPINS!

The Boomer Esiason Foundation is a partnership of leaders in the medical and business communities joining with a committed core of volunteers to provide financial support to research aimed at finding a cure for cystic fibrosis. The Foundation works to heighten education and awareness of cystic fibrosis and to provide a better quality of life for those affected by cystic fibrosis.

Boomer Esiason Foundation
452 Fifth Avenue, Tower 22
New York, NY 10018

Tel: 212-525-7777
Fax: 212-525-0777

Visit the Boomer Esiason Foundation on the Internet at www.esiason.org